CONSENSUS TRANCE

Also read:

THE DOT CONNECTOR LIBRARY, BOOK 1:

Climategate,
The Marijuana Conspiracy,
Project Blue Beam,
and other true stories from The Dot Connector magazine
(2010)

CONSENSUS TRANCE

THE DOT CONNECTOR LIBRARY,
BOOK 2

Published
by Paul Bondarovski

ISBN 978-1-51153-660-8

Contents

Foreword

Most of us live in *consensus trance*, and under "most" I mean almost all of us. Consensus trance is a state of consciousness produced by ideological blunting of our intellect through intensive manipulation (brainwashing), which forces us to accept false conception of reality. And the worst is that we very rarely know if the thoughts in our head are ours or have been skillfully suggested by someone or something else (e.g., subliminals, which can be audio, hidden behind music, or visual, airbrushed into a picture, flashed on a screen so fast that you don't consciously see them, or cleverly incorporated into a picture or design). In the entire history of man, no one has ever been brainwashed and realized, or believed, that he had been brainwashed.

This book is composed of the articles written by different authors at different times, but together they present the Big Picture of mass and individual **mind control** and its various techniques.

Mind control is not only used by the state and the global elite to manipulate us into doing things that we otherwise, if we thought for ourselves, wouldn't ever do (for example, going to war and killing each other all while believing that such a criminal way we are "serving our country"). Unfortunately, if you check books, magazines and websites talking about awakening and spiritual development, many of them are using exactly the same mind control techniques that those evil forces they are supposedly opposing. The fact that they are doing so "for a good purpose" doesn't change anything, because mind control in itself is evil. You cannot control, or even attempt to control the mind of another person and stay a "good" person yourself.

Mind control, in any form and for any purpose, is a crime against human nature and against life itself. It is transforming human beings into remote-controlled robots. It is replacing other people's will with the controller's will; it is making them to become extensions of controller's life and thus depriving them of their natural right to live their own lives. It is theft, because you're taking what is not yours and doing it without another person's knowledge. And it is killing, because it is taking away (literally!) someone else's life.

Five years ago, in 2010, I have published a book with a rather long title, *Climategate, The Marijuana Conspiracy, Project Blue Beam, and other true stories from The Dot Connector magazine* (available from Amazon.com). The magazine that I published then doesn't exist any more, but I have decided to revive its idea in a form of *The Dot Connector Library* series. So, that *Climategate* book can be considered Book 1 of the series, and this is Book 2. Most of the articles have been published in different issues of *The Dot Connector* magazine, some come from other sources, but compiled this way they form a big and unique picture of the subject. For this compilation, the subject is *mind control*.

Paul Bondarovski,
March 2015

Consensus Trance

By Jüri Lina

Our civilization has failed in many crucial areas. These failures have been aggravated by the fact that those who have understood the reason for our troubles refuse to speak out. Others have failed to realize the obvious—that hidden economic forces have acted behind the carefully painted scenes and, virtually unopposed, manipulated us towards our present desperate situation. We have been frightened and weakened, and for this reason the enemies of humanity have succeeded with their treacherous conspiracy.

"Malta yok" is Turkish, a well-known expression among historians, and means "Malta does not exist." In 1565, the Turkish armada discovered enemy ships near Malta. The admirals became so shocked by this that they sent the following message to the Sultan in Istanbul: "Malta yok."

Today independent-minded historians use this expression, when they come across previously inaccessible facts or sensitive historical data, which those in power deny or conceal. There are so many lies mixed with the truth that people get confused. But there is an alternative to the official truth, since things are often not what they seem to be.

In our world, which is controlled by freemasonry, one rule surely applies: if something has happened but is not reported by the mass media, then it has simply not occurred. But if something has not even taken place, and yet is reported in the media, then it has nonetheless happened. We must learn to question the official truth!

Professor Daniel J. Boorstin, Librarian of Congress from 1975 to 1987, once stated: "Americans live in a world of pseudofacts, which is created for them by their own media."

People want to see what does not exist and wish to ignore reality. Life is, therefore, a matter of deception and self-deception. It is difficult to make any progress in this maze of myths. And we certainly live in a labyrinth of lies. It is difficult for many people to orientate themselves since they have not developed their powers of discrimination, that is the ability to distinguish good from evil. This is the reason why the freemasons have been so effective in deluding us with their so-called social ideologies. These lies are dutifully amplified by the megaphones of the mass media, which also attempt to silence, withhold or, as a last resort, mock all information and ideas that do not comply with their propaganda...

Charles T. Tart, professor of psychology at University of California, called this ideological blunting of our intellect *"consensus trance."*[1] Consensus means general agreement or understanding. Consensus trance thus implies the fact that we have accepted false conception of reality, not through logical processing of facts but through intensive manipulation (brainwashing) by the global elite.

Too many of us have been affected by consensus trance, which thus is a common belief in these myths. The methods of suggestion that the freemasons and others manipulators have used in order to make us believe in their lies without second thought have successfully turned most of us into victims of this audacious manipulation. For this reason, we instinctively shy away from uncomfortable facts, which threaten to demolish the false view of the world the freemasons have created and thereby awaken us from the trance. Many of us have been affected by mental paralysis.

But belief is a desire not to know, as the freemason and philosopher Friedrich Nietzsche stated. This is why it is important to expose the most dangerous propaganda myths. The mental anesthetization of the Western world has been a great success. Most people have be-

---

1. Charles T. Tart. *Waking Up: Overcoming the Obstacles to Human Potential.* Boston, 1987.

come victims of the type of blind faith called "political correctness" and prefer to live in their illusory world.

The authorities have invented or exploited certain myths which serve their purposes and work against us. These fantasies apply to history, health, culture, politics and other important subjects. One must have both faith and trust in oneself to find the strength to face the reality that is presented in this book.

Waking up from the trance is a difficult and laborious process. Certain key facts are necessary in order to achieve this, facts which the reader, despite all the lies, can recognize and has a possibility to verify. Here is a classic example from Darwin's journals.

The Patagonians (a tribal people in South Argentina) could not see Darwin's ship, *The Beagle*, conceptually or even optically, since no large ships had hitherto been a part of their experience. Only the shaman of the tribe could see the ship. When the shaman began to describe the ship with the aid of objects known to the Patagonians, the ship became visible to all. They had a consensus reality which applied to small boats but lacked a similar conception of large ships…

Many of us lack critical judgment concerning our social, political and practical environment, since we blindly trust the myths that masonic sources feed us with through the mass media every day.

Most of us who prefer blindly to trust different political, social and scientific fabrications and deny any suggestion about hidden control behind the scenes do not want to see that the most important political, economic and social events in the world are not haphazard, but planned by non-democratic groups who hide behind the name "freemasons." The inferior and degrading conditions, which we see everywhere in different countries, did not just happen to turn out that way. If we accept this explanation, we immediately begin to understand everything that is happening and all the pieces of the jigsaw fall into place. Otherwise we will grope in darkness and understand nothing.

The masonic mythomaniacs are enemies of the spiritual freedom of mankind. Several powerful and ruthless masonic lodges consisting of self-appointed elites during the last two centuries have been steering our society towards certain ruin. If we refuse to see this reality, it means that we accept living in a world without sense, an absurd world, which without any sensible reason has been transformed into a surreal, Kafkaesque lunatic asylum.

These powerful lodges, among other things, worked towards creating a superstate in Europe—the European Union—and are working towards creating a world government under their power by means of psychological warfare against us, the non-masons. These groups undermine the most important dimension in our lives—the spiritual dimension. They have caused the greatest spiritual crisis through the ages. The society the freemasons have formed has lost sight of the true purpose of life. Many people can no longer understand spiritual values. They do not even know what the word "spiritual" means.

The freemasons are ever more intensive in their propagation of unnatural ideas such as globalism (new internationalism) or mondialism, ostensibly for the reason of promoting the spiritual development of humanity and to build a New World Order. This is an unparalleled deception. In fact, the freemasons intend to build a New Temple of Solomon for us. Why should we live in a world, which allegorically could be regarded as an Israelite temple where certain people are chosen to rule and others are their slaves who will be sacrificed like animals?

The temple that Solomon had built was a slaughterhouse where many animals were sacrificed daily to appease the hunger of Yahweh. The priests were actually butchers who became rich through their gruesome work. According to the Russian professor Lev Gumilev, Yahweh is a terrible fire-demon.[2]

In the Soviet Union, masonic terms typical of the communist movement were used constantly. They wanted to "build a new society" and a "better and brighter future," or they wanted to rebuild the old ("perestroika").

Professor of literature Jiro Imai at the University of Tokyo in the 1920s wrote in his book, *On the World-Wide Secret Society,* that "freemasonry is the most dangerous and subversive secret society."

The Swedish association "Save the Individual" (FRI), which com-

---

2. Lev Gumilev, *The Ethnosphere.* Moscow, 1993, p. 480.

bats sects and "saves" people from authoritarian organizations, has listed the criteria that define a destructive movement:

- False declaration of intention and misleading description when recruiting members.
- Manipulation by psychological methods (mind control) is used during recruitment and indoctrination.
- An all-powerful leader who demands total subjection and claims to have special knowledge and powers.
- The ideology must not be questioned, doubt is something evil, which must be fought.
- The image of reality is black and white: the members are the chosen (good), everything outside of the movement is evil and must be opposed.
- There is a lot of money involved, which sometimes emanates from crime.

International freemasonry complies with all these criteria of a destructive sect, but FRI refuses to criticize freemasonry and instead slanders those who expose political freemasonry.

The most dangerous sect of them all, freemasonry has not detached itself from society, but intervenes in its development in a very negative way. Presumably, the freemasons have succeeded in their indoctrination of society, since they are no longer regarded as a serious threat. The masons are in control of the mass media.

"If one controls radio, press, school, church, art, science, film— one can transform each truth into a lie, each unreason into reason," wrote Alf Ahlberg in his book *The Ideals and Their Shadows*.[3] The masses have always believed in those gods that propagate themselves most dramatically.

> The power to control the news flow is the same thing as the power to control how people think. We boast about free press in the United

---

3. Alf Ahlberg, *Idealen och deras skuggbilder/The Ideals and Their Shadows*. Stockholm, 1936, p. 135.

States. But how free is it really when we receive the same news from all the big media conglomerates and when alternative opinions never reach the majority of Americans? The power to report and describe reality is now in the hands of a few. And the interest of these few powerful people is in opposition to the interest of the people, the general interest. It makes no difference that these media conglomerates have different names and appearances, since they all share the same values, which is a guarantee that we receive cloned information. (*The Nation*, as reported by *Aftonbladet*, 31 October 1997.)

The few who control the flow of information belong to international freemasonry. These forces do not care about the interests of the people. Noam Chomsky wrote: "Propaganda works more effectively if one manages to maintain the illusion that the mass media are non-partial observers. Tough debates within invisible boundaries will actually have the effect of strengthening the system."

It is not possible to control masonic lodges or other elite structures. We know that a group which cannot be controlled immediately begins to manipulate the press and believes that it stands above the law. The freemasons use myths as the base of their power in their war against mankind.

Myths as a Base of Power

For centuries, the whole of Europe believed in witches. Huge books written by learned men, such as the infamous *Malleus maleficarum* (*The Witch Hammer*) by Heinrich Institoris and Jakob Sprenger, published in 1486 and printed in further thirty editions until 1669, stigmatized the nefarious practices of witches. This was reason enough for the Church to consider itself justified in executing thousands of innocent women. Would not all of us still believe in witches today if we had been brought up with horror stories about witches from our earliest childhood and if the mass media reported their heinous crimes day after day?

More and more myths have begun to erode recently. They do not stand up to close scrutiny.

The children of Israel were never slaves in Egypt. Neither did they roam through the desert of Sinai for forty years nor conquer the land of Canaan by force. This was revealed by Zeev Herzog, professor of archaeology at the University of Tel Aviv. "The biblical epoch has never occurred. After 70 years of excavations, the archaeologists have reached a frightening conclusion: it is simply not true," Herzog wrote in the Israeli newspaper *Ha'aretz*. Most Israeli archaeologists agree on the fact that the biblical Exodus from Egypt does not correspond to historical facts. Experts have also accepted that Joshua did not conquer the town of Jericho in a single battle and that the town walls did not fall at the blast of trumpets. The archaeologist Adam Zertel at the University of Haifa also knows that the wandering in the desert is a myth. According to Herzog, David and Solomon never ruled over a mighty empire, it was just a little tribal kingdom without any power. Jerusalem, which was captured by King David, was just a feudal estate.

It is generally believed that the Vandals were uncivilized barbarians who destroyed everything in their path. This is a deliberate lie. The Vandals, a Nordic people originated in North Jutland, in southern Scandinavia, were no less civilized than any other people. The Catholic Church opposed the religious beliefs of the Vandals, called Aryanism, which denied the divine nature of Jesus Christ and interpreted all events in the light of the theory of reincarnation. Because of this, the Vandals were a threat to the generally accepted myths. In 534, Byzantium managed to destroy the kingdom of the Vandals with its rich culture and capture their capital city, Carthage. The conquerors killed the aged and children; the men were forced to become soldiers and the women were married to men from other races. After just one generation, the Vandals and their religion had been erased from the face of the Earth. And history is written by the victors.

Not long ago, the Swiss believed that the storming of the Habsburg castles occurred after the taking of oaths in Riitli in 1291. Excavations have shown that the castles were abandoned without a struggle long before, respectively long after 1291. The storming of the castles never happened.[4]

---

4. Werner Meyer, *1291: Die Geschichte*. Allprint, Switzerland, 1991.

The British astrophysicist Fred Hoyle reached the conclusion that the Universe is governed by a greater intelligence. In 1978, Hoyle described the Charles Darwin's theory of evolution as wrong and claimed that the belief that the first living cell was created in the "sea of life" was just as erroneous. In his book, *Evolution from Space*,[5] he distanced himself completely from Darwinism. He stated that "natural selection" could not explain evolution.

Hoyle asked in his book, *The Intelligent Universe:* "Life as we know it is, among other things, dependent on at least 2000 different enzymes. How could the blind forces of the primal sea manage to put together the correct chemical elements to build enzymes?"[6] According to his calculations, the likelihood of this happening is only one in 10 to the 40,000 power (1 followed by 40,000 zeros). That is about the same chance as throwing 50,000 sixes in a row with a die. Or, as Hoyle describes it: "The chance that higher life forms might have emerged in this way is comparable with the chance that a tornado sweeping through a junk-yard might assemble a Boeing 747 from the materials therein... I am at a loss to understand biologists' widespread compulsion to deny what seems to me to be obvious."[7]

The odds are only for enzymes if all other relevant molecules for life are also taken account of in our calculation, the situation for conventional biology becomes intrinsically insuperable. The unique qualities of man (conscience, morals, religion) do not correspond at all to the evolutionary thesis of "the survival of the fittest." A martyr chooses death rather than forsaking his beliefs. Hoyle stressed that science must once again accept that there is a greater intelligence in the Universe. He believes that Darwin's evolutionary theory is a damaging myth. He stated: "We must adjust ourselves to this in our scientific research programs."

The theory of evolution was worked out by the Lunar Society founded on the initiative of the high-ranking freemason Benjamin Franklin in Birmingham, England, in 1765. He later emigrated to

5. Fred Hoyle, *Evolution from Space*. Enslow Publishers, 1982.
6. Fred Hoyle, *The Intelligent Universe*. M. Joseph, 1983.
7. "Hoyle on Evolution", *Nature*, Vol. 294, 12 November 1981, p. 105.

America. The members gathered once a month at the full moon. The society was a revolutionary masonic organization that supported the overthrow of monarchies and undermining the belief in God.[8]

An important member of the Lunar Society was Erasmus Darwin (1731–1802). He became the grandfather of Charles Darwin and between 1794–96 wrote the book *Zoonomia, or the Laws of Organic Life*, the conclusion of which was the same as that of *The Origin of Species*, which his grandson wrote in 1859.

In this way, the freemasons managed to spread misinformation about how we only live one life on Earth and that we are alone in the Universe, which created itself out of nothing. According to humanists, all human development ends with physical death. Darwin's *The Origin of Species* is a fraud. The word "evolution" first appeared only in the sixth edition, printed in 1872. In his book, *In the Minds of Men: Darwin and the New World Order*, the scientist Ian T. Taylor revealed how the Lunar Society and other masonic organizations have led many intellectuals astray with their manipulations and with the aid of "modern science." Both Erasmus Darwin and his friend James Watt in the Lunar Society were freemasons. The older Darwin was initiated into St. David's Lodge No. 36 in Edinburgh in 1754. He later also became a member of Canongate Kilwinning Lodge No. 2.[9]

Scientists now admit that the Neanderthals were not our forebears, since the DNA analysis of the mitochondria shows that they belonged to another species altogether. Svante Pääbo, professor of biology at Munich University, proved that they were not our ancestors.[10]

Charles Darwin later developed an ideology, called humanism, which international freemasonry began to utilize as a weapon against people with spiritual beliefs. Charles Darwin was just an errand boy for the masonic elite. With the help of "humanistic" organizations, the Freemasons have spread atheism and other false doctrines.

The British quantum physicist Paul Davies, however, postulates in

---

8. Ian T. Taylor, *In the Minds of Men: Darwin and the New World Order.* Minneapolis, 1984, p. 55.

9. *Freemasonry Today*, autumn 1999.

10. *Natur & Vetenskap,* No. 9, 1997, p. 11.

his interesting book, *God & the New Physics,*[11] that "a ruling Universal Consciousness utilizes the laws of nature for a determined purpose." In his opinion, quantum physics is the surest way to find God today. Paul Davies writes in an article:

> The very fact that the Universe is in the process of creation and that its laws have allowed complex structures to come into existence and develop into conscious life, is for me a strong testimony that **something is happening** behind the scenes. I find it impossible to deny the impression that everything is planned...[12]

Sigmund Freud's theory of psychoanalysis was just a huge bluff. This was revealed by, among others, Daniel Stern, an American professor of psychiatry in Geneva. Freud's so-called regressive model is not true, Stern claims. If it were true, it would be possible to use it to predict people's problems or to show a connection between early disturbances and problems later in life. But this has not been successful.[13]

Freud belonged to the Jewish masonic organization B'nai B'rith.[14] During the period when Freud was working on his theory of psychoanalysis (1880–1890), he used cocaine daily. Cocaine is a powerful sexual stimulant. He praised the drug and handed it out to friends and acquaintances; he even wrote "songs of praise" in its honor. Freud introduced cocaine to the Western world.

Information about effective political alternatives is concealed from us. The official history is that life was more difficult in the past. But well-functioning political systems have existed, which have not been advertised.

Pharaoh Amenophis IV, who ruled between 1353 and 1335 B.C., was a wise and kind-hearted ruler who seriously tried to reform Egyptian society. He abolished blood sacrifices and converted to the cult of the Sun by only worshiping one god—Aton. He took the name

---

11. Paul Davies, *God & the New Physics.* Pelican, 1984.
12. *Svenska Dagbladet,* 3 March 1989, p. 14.
13. *Svenska Dagbladet,* 1 June 1990.
14. Peter Gay, *Freud.* Papermac, 1989.

Akhenaton ("He who is useful to Aton"). He enjoyed philosophy and detested war. He passed a law, in which he declared that religion stood for goodness and love. He stressed: "The name of our God is Aton, who is the Sun, the great giver of life. Let all people be equal in life as in death."

He moved the capital from Thebes to Tell-Amarna, 300 km to the north, and renamed it Akhet-Aton. He confiscated the property of the priesthood, which had led them to detest the people and to create a state within the state. He divided up the land of the priests among farmers and slaves. He made it illegal to become rich without working. He took all the gold from the temples and gave it to the poor. He regarded poverty as a sign of inefficiency. He released all slaves and personally lived in a modest and frugal way. He made it illegal to slaughter animals by means that led to unnecessary suffering. He stopped all wars and released a large part of the army. Syria, which had become infamous for bringing prostitution and other sins into Egypt, was the first colony to receive independence.

Akhenaton was the victim of a conspiracy. His own doctor poisoned him. His last words were: "The eternal kingdom has no place on Earth. Everything returns to its original form. Fear, hatred and injustice rule the world again and the people will slave and suffer again as they did in past times. It would have been better if I had never been born than that I should live to see evil triumph over good."

Tutankhamun, who took over the throne, returned everything to the old ways.[15] Akhenaton's name was erased from all inscriptions and his royal city was leveled to the ground.

A system based on spirituality can be very successful. This was proved by the Greek mathematician and philosopher Pythagoras (c. 570–c. 495 B.C.), who was from the island of Samos. After his explorative expeditions, he founded the society of Kroton (now Crotone) and the esoteric hylozoist Brotherhood (the association of Pythagoreans) and school in Syracuse, on Sicily. He implemented a just law. The Pythagoreans were the spiritual aristocracy. Besides

---

15. Otto Neubert, *Tutankhamun and the Valley of the Kings.* Manchester, 1954, pp. 151-174.

philosophy and geometry, they seek a numerical basis for the Universe. Pythagoras developed an esoteric school of thought which still exists today.

Pythagoras astonished everyone with his great knowledge of magic. His influence on the development of southern Italy during more than 30 years was extensive. The Pythagoreans reformed society by ethical means. Their government was called the "aristocracy" (the rule of the best or the most knowledgeable). A city-state polis was founded at Kroton which was ruled by 300 aristocrats who were celibate to avoid nepotism. The economy flourished and the cultural life was rich. There was freedom of speech. The central principle was honesty. The women in this system were equal to the men and were permitted to reach high positions in society, as Diogenes Laertius has related.

In Russia, criminal masonic groups seized power in 1917 and founded the opposite of aristocracy—a cacistocracy, the rule of the worst and most ignorant.

Pythagoras' most famous disciple, Plato, developed his theory of the ideal republic from experiences in Crotona. It has been claimed that this theory was the prototype for communism. This is a typical case of misinformation. It was quite the opposite! Plato called for the rule of the philosophers (the wise), not a tyranny of the ignorant.

A rich, jealous, and amoral potentate called Kylon organized a plot against the freethinking aristocrats in Crotona, which led to the execution of many leading philosophers. Pythagoras was forced to flee. Despite this, the influence of the Pythagoreans became even greater after these events. Later, a more extensive revolt was brought about, when many political leaders were killed and many of the schools of the Brotherhood were destroyed (including those in Crotone and Syracuse). The Brotherhood moved from southern Italy to Athens. Information about this golden period of enlightenment has been ignored in modern history.

It was Pythagoras who began to use the term "philosophy" and called himself a philosopher, or "friend of wisdom." Pythagoras also developed an esoteric system called hylozoism. He claimed that all matter possesses consciousness or a soul. All the worlds are spiritual entities. Even the planets are living beings. The Universe is also conscious. Hylozoism in Greek means "the doctrine of living matter" (*hylē* means matter, and *zōos* living, alive).

The spiritual principle seeks to attain more knowledge and less faith. For this reason, the Buddhists believe that the greatest sin is ignorance, because it leads to crime.

No great leaps occur during normal evolution. Revolutions are damaging, especially those brought about to arrest development. This is a serious crime against nature.

Gagarin Was Never in Space

A Soviet propaganda hoax has been revealed in the former communist countries—Hungary, Estonia and Poland. It was a myth that everyone had really believed in that the Soviet Air Force officer Yuri Gagarin had made a space flight. Many Western governments were aware of this Soviet bluff, but did not want to reveal the truth. It was not intended for the people to know that the Soviet Union was a backward state.

One interesting book about this is *Gagarin: A Cosmic Lie?*[16] by the Hungarian journalist István Nemere…

Until 1961, the United States had managed to send up 42 satellites, the Soviet Union only 12. The United States also informed the world that Alan Shepard would make a space journey in the spacecraft *Freedom 7* on 5 May 1961. The Soviet Union was forced to do something to save face. For this reason, a Soviet cosmonaut Vladimir Ilyushin was sent up into space on 7 April 1961. The Americans intercepted several radio communications between him and the space center in the Soviet Union. Ilyushin's landing failed and he was seriously injured. He could not be shown to the public. It was claimed that he had been injured in a car accident. He was sent to China to receive better medical treatment.

The Russian TV documentary, *Cosmonaut Cover-Up* (2001), also claims that, on 7 April 1961, Vladimir Ilyushin left for space, got into

---

16. Nemere István, *Gagarin = kozmikus hazugság?* Danubius Kódex Kiadó, 1990.

trouble during the first orbit, and crash-landed in China during the third orbit. Ilyushin was badly injured and was repatriated to the Soviet Union about a year later. Soon after that he was killed in an engineered car accident.

The Soviet Union did not have a spare capsule at that time, and in Moscow it was decided to orchestrate a huge bluff, "a cosmic lie." Radio Moscow claimed that a Soviet cosmonaut, Yuri Gagarin, had been sent up into space on the morning of 12 April 1961 with the space rocket *Vostok*. According to the official announcement, he had already landed and was in fine health. The whole world believed this, except for the Western intelligence services—they had not managed to register any radio communication between Gagarin and the space center.

This hoax was sloppily orchestrated. Polish newspapers report already on the morning of 12 April that a Soviet cosmonaut had been in space. Newspapers in other countries did not report Gagarin's flight until 13 April.

In a book written for the West, Soviet propagandists claimed that simple peasants recognized Yuri Gagarin soon after he landed in a field and enthusiastically shouted: "Gagarin, Gagarin!" But nothing about his "space journey" had been reported at that time, no pictures of him had been published, and his name had not been mentioned. The message from radio and TV was sent out 35 minutes after the alleged flight. Were the peasants psychic?

The newspaper *Sovetskaya Rossiya* claimed that Gagarin was wearing a *blue* flightsuit when he landed. In his memoirs, Gagarin himself wrote he was dressed in an *orange* flightsuit.

At his press conference, Gagarin read from notes when he "related" his journey. During the press conference, he made several crucial mistakes. He stated that weightlessness was no problem, everything seemed "just normal." We now know that this was not the case. The cosmonaut German Titov, for example, had difficulties with his balance and had heart problems. American astronauts experienced similar symptoms. Gagarin then made his most serious mistake despite the fact that he was constantly assisted by experts who often spoke about "discoveries" in space. He said, "Then I saw South America." This is impossible. At that time, it was night in South America, which meant that it could not be seen at all. According to the official reports, Gagarin began his "journey" at 9:07 AM, Moscow time. He was supposed to have flown over South America at 9:22 AM, Moscow time. In Chile (Santiago), the time would have been 2:22 AM, and in Brazil (Brasília) 3:22 AM. But he could never have reached South America in 15 minutes—for other cosmonauts, it took 45 minutes.

Foreign journalists wondered: "When will the photographs that Gagarin took in space be published?" Gagarin was silent, thought for a moment, and answered: "I didn't have a camera with me!" Even unmanned Soviet space probes had photographic equipment onboard. It would have been an important propaganda triumph to publish Gagarin's pictures from space. The Soviet Union would never have missed an opportunity like that. Shepard's pictures were cabled out immediately. Parts of his flight were also shown on TV.

When Gagarin wanted to travel in space for real in 1968, he was "disposed of," according to István Nemere. On 27 March 1968, his plane exploded. The official report concerning this event contained many contradictions. The report was classified during the communist period. It claimed that there was not much left of Gagarin's body after the crash. In that case, how did his flightsuit come to land in the top of a tree?

There are far too many questions surrounding Gagarin's spaceflight in April 1961.

On 12 April 2001, the Russian senior engineer Mikhail Rudenko, at the Experimental Design Office 456 in Khimki, Moscow region, admitted in *Pravda* that three cosmonauts had died in space before Gagarin was sent up, namely, Alexei Ledovskikh (1957), Serenti Zhaborin (February 1958), and Andrei Mitkov (flight attempt January 1959). The Russian journalist and cosmonaut candidate (June 1965) Yaroslav Golovanov (1932–2003) wrote in his book, *Cosmonaut One*, that, on 10 November 1960, another cosmonaut, Byelokonyev, also died onboard a spaceship in orbit. Several sources reveal that 7 to 11 cosmonauts have died in orbit before Gagarin.

The NASA knew about the Gagarin bluff, but said nothing. Instead, they have come up with more and more ridiculous lies themselves. It is claimed that those astronauts who were freemasons performed magic rituals in space. In the Grand Lodge of Dallas, there is a painting of American astronauts on the Moon performing certain secret masonic rituals. According to official information, the American astronaut and freemason Edwin Aldrin left the banner of the Knights Templar on the surface of the Moon. It was also claimed that two gold rings were left on the Moon, the purpose of which has not been clarified. Information was later "leaked" that the freemasons attempted to contact the demons on the Moon with the aid of these gold rings. Kenneth Kleinknecht, a department head at NASA as well as a high-ranking freemason and a member of the secretariat within the Scottish Rite, supposedly issued the orders for these rituals.[17] The masonic leaders have a very strange perception of reality.

The documentary *What Happened on the Moon?* by the famous photographer David S. Percy shows that we have every reason to doubt the authenticity of the manned *Apollo* flights. The film shows in detail how the pictures "from the Moon" in conjunction with the first flight on 20 July 1969 (*Apollo* 11) were falsified. Shadows fall in different directions, which suggests artificial lighting (which has been officially denied). In pictures taken from different places the astronauts were not in darkness even when they were in the shade; the same background was used and the same hill appeared twice during two different landings. Despite the clear view, no stars were visible in the sky; no crater formed under the lunar landing module where the rocket thrusters had braked; no dust had settled on the landing module and its struts; the flag waved despite the fact that there is no atmosphere on the Moon; the sound of engines (150 decibels) was missing in the NASA film, yet it was possible to hear the astronauts' voices. A "moon rock" with a "G" marked on it could be seen (as if it was a marked prop). A Coca-Cola bottle was visible on the TV screen (perhaps they sell them on the Moon?), the TV signal did not come

---

17. Michael A. Hoffman II, *Secrets of Masonic Mind Control*, Dresden, NY, 1989, p. 40.

from the Moon, but from Australia, and the Earth was visible from the windows on both sides of the space capsule.

It was technically impossible at that time to perform a lunar landing. (Bill Kaysing, a technician at the company who built the *Apollo* rockets, claimed that the chance of reaching the Moon and returning safely was around 0.017 percent.) Upon leaving the Moon, no flames were seen coming from the rocket's engine, as if wires had pulled up the rocket. A few months before the alleged trip to the Moon, a prototype of the landing module was tested. Neil Armstrong lost control of the module at a height of 90 meters, but managed to eject himself. How is it that the lunar landing went perfectly?

Astronauts cannot travel to the Moon because of the radiation in the Van Allen belts; inner belt is approximately 2,400–5,600 km distant from the Earth and 3,200 kilometers wide, outer belt is 12,000–19,000 km distant from the Earth. This radiation was discovered with the aid of satellite sensors in 1958. Charged particles, protons and electrons, which have been caught in the Earth's magnetic field, move about rapidly in these belts. These particles have been created within the Earth's atmosphere by cosmic radiation and solar winds (corpuscular radiation). They move simultaneously in three different patterns: in spirals around the magnetic line, back and forth along the magnetic line, and in orbit around the Earth; electrons move from west to east, protons from east to west. The most dangerous particles, which contain most energy, have collected in the inner parts of the belts, an area which astronauts absolutely must avoid. If an astronaut passed through these belts, he would become seriously ill or die from the radiation shortly after exposure. The photographs that were taken would likewise have been destroyed. During magnetic solar storms, the radiation increases. On such occasions it can be a thousand times stronger than usual. The *Apollo 16* mission coincided with the most intensive solar storm ever. A two-meter layer of lead would have been necessary to protect the astronauts, according to the physicist Ralph René. The space capsule had a thin shell of aluminium. Due to the radiation, the Russians never even attempted to send anyone to the Moon.

Bill Kaysing believed that the astronauts circled the Earth for eight days and that NASA showed fake pictures of the Moon in the meantime. The pictures were taken in the Nevada desert, at a secret military base called Area 51.

The statistics from the unmanned flights allowed too small a margin for successful flights, whereas the manned flights were nearly exclusively successful. Despite the fact that the electrical system of *Apollo 12* was critically damaged by lightning, it successfully managed to "land on the Moon" using just the reserve system. Only a child could believe in such a fairy tale. When a real attempt was made in 1970 with *Apollo 13*, everything went wrong.

The question is, what is true and what is bluff? At least 25% of Americans believe man has never landed on the Moon. The *Apollo* hoax cost the American taxpayers 40 billion dollars. We will never know what the cost would have been if the U.S. government had really tried to put a man on the Moon.

One thing is certain—you cannot trust the authorities. They are notorious liars and also quite careless.

*   *   *

The freemasons expose us to a palimpsest or codex rescriptus by destroying and concealing the ancient spiritual culture and replacing it with a worthless mass culture, the goal of which is to strengthen the effect of *consensus trance*. During the Middle Ages, expensive vellum was processed for reuse by erasing a part or all of the original text with a pumice stone. Priceless texts from the ancient world were destroyed and replaced by theological drivel. As early as the 18th century, it became possible to expose the original texts with the aid of chemicals. In this way, Cicero's great work, *De re publica,* was recreated.

Unfortunately, most of the people are very susceptible to the poisonous and false ideology of the ruing elite. Today, "politically correct" individuals are hopelessly indoctrinated and may be regarded as "political illiterates" since they are totally ignorant of the hidden reality that controls our lives. Goethe wrote: "Nothing is more terrifying than extreme ignorance." In today's world, information is regarded as "credible" only if it is published by the government-controlled media. Unofficial information from alternative sources is not taken seriously unless it coincides with the official information. As far as history goes, what you think is truth, may just be propaganda.

Updated from issue 5 of The Dot Connector Magazine
(September-October 2009).

The Battle for Your Mind

Persuasion and brainwashing techniques being used on the public today

By Dick Sutphen

This article is an expanded version of a talk Dick Sutphen delivered at the World Congress of Professional Hypnotists Convention in Las Vegas, Nevada. Although the author has been interviewed about the subject on many local and regional radio and TV talk shows, large-scale mass communication appears to be blocked, since it could result in suspicion or investigation of the very media presenting it or the sponsors that support the media. Some government agencies do not want this information generally known.

Everything I will relate only exposes the surface of the problem. I don't know how the misuse of these techniques can be stopped. I don't think it is possible to legislate against that which often cannot be detected. And if those who legislate are using these techniques, there is little hope of affecting laws to govern usage. I do know that the first step to initiate change is to generate interest. In this case, that will probably only result from an underground effort.

In talking about this subject, I am talking about my own business. I know it, and I know how effective it can be.

I produce hypnosis and subliminal apes and, in some of my seminars, I use conversion tactics to assist participants to become independent and self-sufficient. But anytime I use these techniques, I point out that I am using them, and those attending have a choice to participate or not. They also know what the desired result of participation will be.

So, to begin, I want to state the most basic of all facts about brain-washing: *In the entire history of man, no one has ever been brainwashed and realized, or believed, that he had been brainwashed.* Those who have been brainwashed will usually passionately defend their manipulators, claiming they have simply been "shown the light" … or have been transformed in miraculous ways.

The Birth of Conversion

Conversion is a nice word for *brainwashing*, and any study of brainwashing has to begin with a study of Christian revivalism in eighteenth century America.

Apparently, Jonathan Edwards accidentally discovered the techniques during a religious crusade in 1735 in Northampton, Massachusetts. By inducing guilt and acute apprehension and by increasing the tension, the "sinners" attending his revival meetings would break down and completely submit. Technically, what Edwards was doing was creating conditions that wipe the brain slate clean so that the mind accepts new programming. The problem was that the new input was negative. He would tell them, *"You're a sinner! You're destined for hell!"* As a result, one person committed suicide and another attempted suicide. And the neighbors of the suicidal converts related that they, too, were affected so deeply that, although they had found "eternal salvation," they were obsessed with a diabolical temptation to end their own lives.

Once a preacher, cult leader, manipulator or authority figure creates the brain phase to wipe the brain slate clean, his subjects are wide open. New input, in the form of suggestion, can be substituted for their previous ideas. Because Edwards didn't turn his message positive until the end of the revival, many accepted the negative suggestions and acted, or desired to act, upon them.

Charles J. Finney was another Christian revivalist who used the same techniques four years later in mass religious conversions in New York. The techniques are still being used today by Christian revivalists, cults, human potential trainings, some business rallies, and the United States Armed Services—to name just a few.

Let me point out here that I don't think most revivalist preachers realize or know they are using brainwashing techniques. Edwards simply stumbled upon a technique that really worked, and others copied it and have continued to copy it for over two hundred years. And the more sophisticated our knowledge and technology become, the more effective the conversion. I feel strongly that this is one of the major reasons for the increasing rise in Christian fundamentalism, especially the televised variety, while most of the orthodox religions are declining.

The Three Brain Phases

The Christians may have been the first to successfully formulate brainwashing, but we have to look to Pavlov, the Russian scientist, for a technical explanation. In the early 1900s, his work with animals opened the door to further investigations with humans. After the revolution in Russia, Lenin was quick to see the potential of applying Pavlov's research to his own ends.

Three distinct and progressive states of *transmarginal inhibition* were identified by Pavlov.

The first is the *equivalent* phase, in which the brain gives the same response to both strong and weak stimuli.

The second is the *paradoxical* phase, in which the brain responds more actively to weak stimuli than to strong.

And the third is the *ultra-paradoxical* phase, in which conditioned responses and behavior patterns turn from positive to negative or from negative to positive.

With the progression through each phase, the degree of conversion becomes more effective and complete. The ways to achieve conversion are many and varied, but the usual first step in religious or political brainwashing is to work on the emotions of an individual or group until they reach an abnormal level of anger, fear, excitement, or nervous tension. The progressive result of this mental condition is to impair judgment and increase suggestibility. The more this condition can be maintained or intensified, the more it compounds. Once catharsis, or the first brain phase, is reached, the complete mental takeover becomes easier. Existing mental programming can be replaced with new patterns of thinking and behavior.

Other often used physiological weapons to modify normal brain functions are fasting, radical or high sugar diets, physical discomforts, regulation of breathing, mantra chanting in meditation, the disclosure of awesome mysteries, special lighting and sound effects, programmed response to incense, or intoxicating drugs.

The same results can be obtained in contemporary psychiatric treatment by electric shock treatments and even by purposely lowering a person's blood sugar level with insulin injections.

Before I talk about exactly how some of the techniques are applied, I want to point out that hypnosis and conversion tactics are two distinctly different things and that conversion techniques are far more powerful. However, the two are often mixed, with powerful results.

How Revivalist Preachers Work

If you'd like to see a revivalist preacher at work, there are probably several in your city. Go to the church or tent early and sit in the rear, about three-quarters of the way back. Most likely repetitive music will be played while the people come in for the service. A repetitive beat, ideally ranging from 45 to 72 beats per minute (a rhythm close to the beat of the human heart), is very hypnotic and can generate an eyes-open altered state of consciousness in a very high percentage of people. And, once you are in an alpha state, you are at least 25 times as suggestible as you would be in full beta consciousness.

The music is probably the same for every service, or incorporates the same beat, and many of the people will go into an altered state almost immediately upon entering the sanctuary. Subconsciously, they recall their state of mind from previous services and respond according to the post-hypnotic programming.

Watch the people waiting for the service to begin. Many will exhibit external signs of trance—body relaxation and slightly dilated eyes. Often, they begin swaying back and forth with their hands in the air while sitting in their chairs. Next, the assistant pastor will probably come out. He usually speaks with a pretty good "voice roll."

Voice Roll Technique

A "voice roll" is a patterned, paced style used by hypnotists when inducing a trance. It is also used by many lawyers, several of whom are highly trained hypnotists, when they desire to entrench a point firmly in the minds of the jurors. A voice roll can sound as if the speaker were talking to the beat of a metronome, or it may sound as though he were emphasizing every word in a monotonous, patterned style. The words will usually be delivered at the rate of 45 to 60 beats per minute, maximizing the hypnotic effect.

Now the assistant pastor begins the "build-up" process. He induces an altered state of consciousness and/or begins to generate the excitement and the expectations of the audience. Next, a group of young women in "sweet and pure" chiffon dresses might come out to sing a song. Gospel songs are great for building excitement and *involvement*. In the middle of the song, one of the girls might be "smitten by the spirit" and fall down or react as if possessed by the Holy Spirit. This very effectively increases the intensity in the room. At this point, hypnosis and conversion tactics are being mixed. And the result is the audience's attention span is now totally focused upon the communication while the environment becomes more exciting or tense.

Right about this time, when an eyes-open mass-induced alpha mental state has been achieved, they will usually pass the collection plate or basket. In the background, a 45-beat-per-minute voice roll from the assistant preacher might exhort, *"Give to God! Give to God! Give to God!"* And the audience does give. God may not get the money, but his already wealthy representative will.

Next, the fire-and-brimstone preacher will come out. He induces fear and increases the tension by talking about "the devil," "going to hell," or the forthcoming Armageddon. In the last such rally I attended, the preacher talked about the blood that would soon be running out of every faucet in the land. He was also obsessed with a *"bloody axe of God,"* which everyone had seen hanging above the pulpit the previous week. I have no doubt that everyone saw it—the power of suggestion given to hundreds of people in hypnosis assures that at least 10 to 25 percent would see whatever he suggested they see.

In most revivalist gatherings, "testifying" or "witnessing" usually follows the fear-based sermon. People from the audience come up on stage and relate their stories. *"I was crippled, and now I can walk!"* *"I had arthritis, and now it's gone!"* It is a psychological manipulation that works. After listening to numerous case histories of miraculous healings, the average guy in the audience with a minor problem is sure he can be healed. The room is charged with fear, guilt, intense excitement, and expectations. Now those who want to be healed are frequently lined up around the edge of the room, or they are told to come down to the front. The preacher might touch them on the head firmly and scream, *"Be healed!"* This releases the psychic energy and, for many, catharsis results. Catharsis is a purging of repressed emotions. Individuals might cry, fall down or even go into spasms. And if catharsis is effected, they stand a chance of being healed. In catharsis (one of the three brain phases mentioned earlier), the brain slate is temporarily wiped clean and the new suggestion is accepted.

For some, the healing may be permanent. For many, it will last four days to a week, which is, incidentally, how long a hypnotic suggestion given to a somnambulistic subject will usually last. Even if the healing doesn't last, if they come back every week, the power of suggestion may continually override the problem; or sometimes, sadly, it can mask a physical problem, which could prove to be very detrimental to the individual in the long run. I'm not saying that legitimate healings do not take place. They do. Maybe the individual was ready to let go of the negativity that caused the problem in the first place; maybe it was the work of God. Yet, I contend that it can be explained with existing knowledge of brain/mind function.

The techniques and staging will vary from church to church. Many use "speaking in tongues" to generate catharsis in some while the spectacle creates intense excitement in the observers. The use of hypnotic techniques by religions is sophisticated, and professionals are assuring that they become even more effective. A man in Los Angeles is designing, building, and reworking a lot of churches around the country. He tells ministers what they need and how to use it. This man's track record indicates that the congregation and the monetary income will double if the minister follows his instructions. He admits that about 80 percent of his efforts are in the sound system and lighting. Powerful sound and the proper use of lighting are of primary importance in inducing an altered state of consciousness—I've been using them for years in my own seminars. However, my participants are fully aware of the process and what they can expect as a result of their participation.

Six Conversion Techniques

Cults and human potential organizations are always looking for new converts. To attain them, they must also create a brain phase. And they often need to do it within a short space of time—a weekend, or maybe even a day. The following are the six primary techniques used to generate the conversion.

The meeting or training takes place in an area where participants are cut off from the outside world. This may be any place: a private home, a remote or rural setting, or even a hotel ballroom where the participants are allowed only limited bathroom usage. In human potential trainings, the controllers will give a lengthy talk about the importance of *"keeping agreements"* in life. The participants are told that if they don't keep agreements, their life will never work. It's a good idea to keep agreements, but the controllers are subverting a positive human value for selfish purposes. The participants vow to themselves and their trainer that they will keep their agreements. Anyone who does not will be intimidated into agreement or forced to leave.

The next step is to agree to complete training, thus assuring a high percentage of conversions for the organizations. They will *usually* have to agree not to take drugs, smoke, and sometimes not to eat; or they are given such short meal breaks that it creates tension. The real reason for the agreements is to alter internal chemistry, which generates anxiety and hopefully causes at least a slight malfunction of the nervous system, which in turn increases the conversion potential. Before the gathering is complete, the agreements will be used to ensure that the new converts go out and find new participants. They are intimidated into agreeing to do so before they leave. Since the importance of keeping agreements is so high on their priority list, the converts will twist the arms of everyone they know, attempting to talk them into attending a free introductory session offered at a future date by the organization.

The new converts are zealots. In fact, the inside term for merchandising the largest and most successful human potential training is, *"Sell it by zealot!"* At least a million people are graduates and a good percentage have been left with a mental activation button that assures their future loyalty and assistance if the guru figure or organization calls. Think about the potential political implications of hundreds of thousands of zealots programmed to campaign for their guru.

Be wary of an organization of this type that offers follow-up sessions after the seminar. Follow-up sessions might be weekly meetings or inexpensive seminars given on a regular basis which the organization will attempt to talk you into taking; or any regularly scheduled event used to maintain control. As the early Christian revivalists found, long-term control is dependent upon a good follow-up system.

All right. Now, let's look at the second tip-off that indicates conversion tactics are being used. A schedule is maintained that causes physical and mental fatigue. This is primarily accomplished by long hours in which the participants are given no opportunity for relaxation or reflection.

The third tip-off: techniques used to increase the tension in the room or environment.

Number four: uncertainty. I could spend hours relating various techniques to increase tension and generate uncertainty. Basically, the participants are concerned about being "put on the spot" or encountered by the trainers, guilt feelings are played upon, participants are tempted to verbally relate their innermost secrets to the other participants or forced to take part in activities that emphasize removing their masks.

One of the most successful human potential seminars forces the participants to stand on a stage in front of the entire audience while being verbally attacked by the trainers. A public opinion poll, conducted a few years ago, showed that the number one most fearful situation an individual could encounter is to speak to an audience. It ranked above window washing outside the 85th floor of an office building. So you can imagine the fear and tension this situation generates within the participants. Many faint, but most cope with the stress by mentally going away. They literally go into an alpha state, which automatically makes them many times as suggestible as they normally are. And another loop of the downward spiral into conversion is successfully effected.

The fifth clue that conversion tactics are being used is the introduction of jargon—new terms that have meaning only to the "insiders" who participate. Vicious language is also frequently used, purposely, to make participants uncomfortable.

The final tip-off is that there is no humor in the communications, at least until the participants are converted. Then, merry-making and humor are highly desirable as symbols of the new joy the participants have supposedly "found."

I'm not saying that good does not result from participation in such gatherings. It can and does. But I contend it is important for people to know what has happened and to be aware that continual involvement may not be in their best interest.

Over the years, I've conducted professional seminars to teach people to be hypnotists, trainers, and counselors. I've had many of those who conduct trainings and rallies come to me and say, *"I'm here because I know that what I'm doing works, but I don't know why."* After showing them how and why, many have gotten out of the business or have decided to approach it differently or in a much more loving and supportive manner.

Many of these trainers have become personal friends, and it scares us all to have experienced the power of one person with a microphone and a room full of people. Add a little charisma, and you can count on a high percentage of conversions. The sad truth is that a high percentage of people want to give away their power—they are "true believers"! Cult gatherings or human potential trainings are an ideal environment to observe first-hand what is technically called the

"Stockholm Syndrome." This is a situation in which those who are intimidated, controlled, or made to suffer, begin to love, admire, and even sometimes sexually desire their controllers or captors.

But let me inject a word of warning here: *if you think you can attend such gatherings and not be affected, you are probably wrong.*

A perfect example is the case of a woman who went to Haiti on a Guggenheim Fellowship to study Haitian Voodoo. In her report, she related how the music eventually induced uncontrollable bodily movement and an altered state of consciousness. Although she understood the process and thought herself above it, when she began to feel herself become vulnerable to the music, she attempted to fight it and turned away. Anger or resistance almost always assures conversion. A few moments later she was possessed by the music and began dancing in a trance around the Voodoo meeting house. A brain phase had been induced by the music and excitement, and she awoke feeling reborn.

The only hope of attending such gatherings without being affected is to be a Buddha and allow no positive or negative emotions to surface. Few people are capable of such detachment.

Before I go on, let's go back to the six tip-offs to conversion. I want to mention the United States government and military boot camp. The Marine Corps talks about breaking men down before "rebuilding" them as new men—as marines! Well, that is exactly what they do, the same way a cult breaks its people down and rebuilds them as happy flower sellers on your local street corner. Every one of the six conversion techniques are used in boot camp. Considering the needs of the military, I'm not making a judgment as to whether that is good or bad. *It is a fact* that the men are effectively brainwashed. Those who won't submit must be discharged or spend much of their time in the brig.

Decognition Process

Once the initial conversion is effected, cults, armed services, and similar groups cannot have cynicism among their members. Members must respond to commands and do as they are told, otherwise they are dangerous to the organizational control. This is normally accomplished as a three-step *decognition process.*

STEP ONE is *alertness reduction*: The controllers cause the nervous system to malfunction, making it difficult to distinguish between fantasy and reality. This can be accomplished in several ways. *Poor diet* is one; watch out for Brownies and Koolaid. The sugar throws the nervous system off. More subtle is the *"spiritual diet"* used by many cults. They eat only vegetables and fruits; without the grounding of grains, nuts, seeds, dairy products, fish or meat, an individual becomes mentally "spacey." *Inadequate sleep* is another primary way to reduce alertness, especially when combined with long hours of work or intense physical activity. Also, being bombarded with intense and unique experiences achieves the same result.

STEP TWO is *programmed confusion*: You are mentally assaulted while your alertness is being reduced as in Step One. This is accomplished with a deluge of new information, lectures, discussion groups, encounters or one-to-one processing, which usually amounts to the controller bombarding the individual with questions. During this phase of decognition, reality and illusion often merge and perverted logic is likely to be accepted.

STEP THREE is *thought stopping*: Techniques are used to cause the mind to go "flat." These are altered-state-of-consciousness techniques that initially induce calmness by giving the mind something simple to deal with and focusing awareness. The continued use brings on a feeling of elation and eventually hallucination. The result is the reduction of thought and eventually, if used long enough, the cessation of all thought and withdrawal from everyone and everything except that which the controllers direct. The takeover is then complete. It is important to be aware that when members or participants are instructed to use "thought stopping" techniques, they are told that they will benefit by so doing: they will become "better soldiers" or "find enlightenment."

There are three primary techniques used for thought stopping.

The first is *marching*: the thump, thump, thump beat literally generates self-hypnosis and thus great susceptibility to suggestion.

The second thought stopping technique is *meditation*. If you spend an hour to an hour and a half a day in meditation, after a few weeks, there is a great probability that you will not return to full beta consciousness. You will remain in a fixed state of alpha for as long as you continue to meditate. I'm not saying this is bad—if you do it yourself. It may be very beneficial. But it is a fact that you are causing your mind to go flat. I've worked with meditators on an EEG machine and the results are conclusive: the more you meditate, the flatter your mind becomes until, eventually and especially if used to excess or in combination with decognition, all thought ceases. Some spiritual groups see this as nirvana—which is bullshit. It is simply a predictable physiological result. And if heaven on earth is non-thinking and non-involvement, I really question why we are here.

The third thought stopping technique is *chanting*, and often chanting in meditation. "Speaking in tongues" could also be included in this category. All these thought stopping techniques produce an altered state of consciousness.

This may be very good if *you* are controlling the process, for you also control the input. I personally use at least one self-hypnosis programming session every day and I know how beneficial it is for me. But you need to know, if you use these techniques to the degree of remaining continually in alpha, that, although you'll be very mellow, you'll also be more suggestible.

True Believers and Mass Movements

Before ending this section on conversion, I want to talk about the people who are most susceptible to it and about mass movements. I am convinced that at least a third of the population is what Eric Hoffer calls *"true believers."* They are joiners and followers, people who want to give away their power. They look for answers, meaning and enlightenment outside themselves.

Hoffer, who wrote *The True Believer*, a classic on mass movements, says, *"true believers are not intent on bolstering and advancing a cherished self, but are those craving to be rid of unwanted self. They are followers, not because of a desire for self-advancement, but because it can satisfy their passion for self-renunciation."* Hoffer also says that true believers *"are eternally incomplete and eternally insecure."*

I know this from my own experience. In my years of communicating concepts and conducting trainings, I have run into them again and again. All I can do is attempt to show them that the only thing to seek is the *true self within.* Their personal answers are to be found there, and there alone. I communicate that the basics of spirituality are self-responsibility and self-actualization.

But most of the true believers just tell me that I'm not spiritual and go looking for someone who will give them the dogma and structure they desire.

Never underestimate the potential danger of these people. They can easily be molded into fanatics who will gladly work and die for their "holy cause." It is a substitute for their lost faith in themselves and offers them as a substitute for individual hope.

The Moral Majority is made up of true believers. All cults are composed of true believers. You'll find them in politics, churches, businesses, and social cause groups. They are the fanatics in these organizations.

Mass movements will usually have a charismatic leader. The followers want to convert others to their way of living or impose a new way of life—if necessary, by legislating laws forcing others to their view, as evidenced by the activities of the Moral Majority. This means enforcement by guns or punishment, for that is the bottomline in law enforcement.

A common hatred, enemy, or devil, is essential to the success of a mass movement. The Born-Again Christians have Satan himself, but that isn't enough—they've added the occult, the New Age thinkers and, lately, all those who oppose their integration of church and politics, as evidenced in their political reelection campaigns against those who oppose their views. In revolutions, the devil is usually the ruling power or aristocracy. Some human potential movements are far too clever to ask their graduates to join anything, thus labeling themselves as a cult—but, if you look closely, you'll find that their devil is anyone and everyone who hasn't taken their training.

There are mass movements without devils, but they seldom attain major status. The true believers are mentally unbalanced or insecure people, or those without hope or friends. People don't look for allies when they love, but they do when they hate or become obsessed with a cause. And those who desire a new life and a new order feel the old ways must be eliminated before the new order can be built.

Persuasion Techniques

Persuasion isn't technically brainwashing, but it is the manipulation of the human mind by another individual without the manipulated party being aware what caused his opinion shift. I only have time to very basically introduce you to a few of the thousands of techniques in use today, but the basis of persuasion is always to access your *right brain*. The left half of your brain is analytical and rational. The right side is creative and imaginative. That is overly simplified, but it makes my point. So, the idea is to distract the left brain and keep it busy. Ideally, the persuader generates an eyes-open altered state of consciousness, causing you to shift from beta awareness into alpha; this can be measured on an EEG machine.

First, let me give you an example of distracting the left brain. Politicians use these powerful techniques all the time; lawyers use many variations, which, I've been told, they call *"tightening the noose."*

Assume for a moment that you are watching a politician give a speech. First, he might generate what is called a *"yes set."* These are statements that will cause listeners to agree; they might even unknowingly nod their heads in agreement. Next come the *truisms.* These are usually facts that could be debated but, once the politician has his audience agreeing, the odds are in the politician's favor that the audience won't stop to think for themselves, thus continuing to agree. Last comes the *suggestion.* This is what the politician wants you to do and, since you have been agreeing all along, you could be persuaded to accept the suggestion. Now, if you'll listen closely to my political speech, you'll find that the first three are the "yes set," the next three are truisms, and the last is the suggestion.

"Ladies and gentlemen, are you angry about high food prices? Are

you tired of astronomical gas prices? Are you sick of out-of-control in-flation? Well, you know the Other Party allowed 18 percent inflation last year; you know crime has increased 50 percent nationwide in the last 12 months, and you know your paycheck hardly covers your expenses any more. Well, the answer to resolving these problems is to elect me, John Jones, to the u.s. Senate."

And I think you've heard all that before. But you might also watch for what are called *imbedded commands*. As an example: On key words, the speaker would make a gesture with his left hand which research has shown is more apt to access your right brain. Today's media-oriented politicians and spellbinders are often carefully trained by a whole new breed of specialist who are using every trick in the book—both old and new—to manipulate you into accepting their candidate.

The concepts and techniques of neuro-linguistics are so heavily protected that I found out the hard way that to even talk about them publicly or in print results in threatened legal action. Yet neuro-linguistic training is readily available to anyone willing to devote the time and pay the price. It is some of the most subtle and powerful manipulation I have yet been exposed to. A good friend who recently attended a two-week seminar on neuro-linguistics found that many of those she talked to during the breaks were government people.

Another technique that I'm just learning about is unbelievably slippery; it is called an *interspersal technique* and the idea is to say one thing with words but plant a subconscious impression of something else in the minds of the listeners and/or watchers.

Let me give you an example. Assume you are watching a television commentator make the following statement: *"Senator Johnson is assisting local authorities to clear up the stupid mistakes of companies contributing to the nuclear waste problems."* It sounds like a statement of fact, but, if the speaker emphasizes the right word, and especially if he makes the proper hand gestures on the key words, you could be left with the subconscious impression that Senator Johnson is stupid. That was the subliminal goal of the statement and the speaker cannot be called to account for anything.

Persuasion techniques are also frequently used on a much smaller scale with just as much effectiveness. The insurance salesman knows his pitch is likely to be much more effective if he can get you to visualize something in your mind. This is right-brain communication. For instance, he might pause in his conversation, look slowly around your living room and say, *"Can you just imagine this beautiful home burning to the ground?"* Of course you can! It is one of your unconscious fears and, when he forces you to visualize it, you are more likely to be manipulated into signing his insurance policy.

The Hare Krishnas operating in every airport use what I call *shock and confusion* techniques to distract the left brain and communicate directly with the right brain. While waiting for a plane, I once watched one operate for over an hour. He had a technique of almost jumping in front of someone. Initially, his voice was loud then dropped as he made his pitch to take a book and contribute money to the cause. Usually, when people are shocked, they immediately withdraw. In this case they were shocked by the strange appearance, sudden materialization and loud voice of the Hare Krishna devotee. In other words, the people went into an alpha state for security, because they didn't want to confront the reality before them. In alpha, they were highly suggestible, so they responded to the suggestion of taking the book. The moment they took the book, they felt guilty and responded to the second suggestion: give money. We are all conditioned that if someone gives us something, we have to give them something in return—in that case, it was money. While watching this hustler, I was close enough to notice that many of the people he stopped exhibited an outward sign of alpha—their eyes were actually dilated.

Subliminal Programming

Subliminals are hidden suggestions that only your subconscious perceives. They can be audio, hidden behind music, or visual, airbrushed into a picture, flashed on a screen so fast that you don't consciously see them, or cleverly incorporated into a picture or design.

Most audio subliminal reprogramming tapes offer verbal suggestions recorded at a low volume. I question the efficacy of this technique—if subliminals are not perceptible, they cannot be effective, and subliminals recorded below the audible threshold are therefore useless. The oldest audio subliminal technique uses a voice that follows the volume of the music, so subliminals are impossible to detect without a parametric equalizer. But this technique is patented, and when I wanted to develop my own line of subliminal audio cassettes, negotiations with the patent holder proved to be unsatisfactory. My attorney obtained copies of the patents which I gave to some talented Hollywood sound engineers asking them to create a new technique. They found a way to psycho-acoustically modify and synthesize the suggestions so that they are projected in the same chord and frequency as the music thus giving them the effect of being part of the music. But we found that in using this technique there is no way to reduce various frequencies to detect the subliminals. In other words, although the suggestions are being heard by the subconscious mind, they cannot be monitored with even the most sophisticated equipment.

If we were able to come up with this technique as easily as we did, I can only imagine how sophisticated the technology has become with unlimited government or advertising funding. And I shudder to think about the propaganda and commercial manipulation that we are exposed to on a daily basis. There is simply no way to know what is behind the music you hear. It may even be possible to hide a second voice behind the voice to which you are listening. The series by Wilson Bryan Key, PHD, on subliminals in advertising and political campaigns well documents the misuse in many areas, especially printed advertising in newspapers, magazines, and posters.

The big question about subliminals is: do they work? And I guarantee you they do. Not only from the response of those who have used my tapes, but from the results of such programs as the subliminals behind the music in department stores. Supposedly, the only message is instructions to not steal: one East Coast department store chain reported a 37 percent reduction in thefts in the first nine months of testing.

A 1984 article in the technical newsletter, *Brain-Mind Bulletin*, states that as much as 99 percent of our cognitive activity may be "non-conscious," according to the director of the Laboratory for Cognitive Psychophysiology at the University of Illinois. The lengthy report ends with the statement, *"These findings support the use of subliminal approaches such as taped suggestions for weight loss and the therapeutic use of hypnosis and neuro-linguistic programming."*

Mass Misuse

I could relate many stories that support subliminal programming, but I'd rather use my time to make you aware of even more subtle uses of such programming I have personally experienced sitting in a Los Angeles auditorium with over ten thousand people who were gathered to listen to a current charismatic figure. Twenty minutes after entering the auditorium, I became aware that I was going in and out of an altered state. Those accompanying me experienced the same thing.

Since it is our business, we were aware of what was happening, but those around us were not. By careful observation, what appeared to be spontaneous demonstrations were, in fact, artful manipulations. The only way I could figure that the eyes-open trance had been induced was that a 6 to 7-cycle-per-second vibration was being piped into the room behind the air conditioner sound. That particular vibration generates alpha, which would render the audience highly susceptible. Ten to 25 percent of the population is capable of a somnambulistic level of altered states of consciousness; for these people, the suggestions of the speaker, if non-threatening, could potentially be accepted as "commands."

Vibrato

Vibrato is the tremulous effect imparted in some vocal or instrumental music, and the cycle-per-second range causes people to go into an altered state of consciousness. At one period of English history, singers whose voices contained pronounced vibrato were not allowed to perform publicly, because listeners would go into an altered state and have fantasies, often sexual in nature. People who attend opera or enjoy listening to singers like Mario Lanza are familiar with this altered state induced by the performers.

ELF

Now, let's carry this awareness a little farther. There are also inaudible ELF (extra-low frequency) waves. These are electromagnetic in nature. One of the primary uses of ELF waves is to communicate with our submarines.

Dr. Andrija Puharich, a highly respected researcher, in an attempt to warn U.S. officials about Russian use of ELF waves, set up an experiment. Volunteers were wired so their brain waves could be measured on an EEG. They were sealed in a metal room that could not be penetrated by a normal signal. Puharich then beamed ELF waves at the volunteers. ELF waves go right through the earth and, of course, through metal walls. Those inside couldn't know if the signal was or was not being sent. Puharich watched the reactions on the technical equipment: 30 percent of those inside the room were taken over by the ELF signal in six to ten seconds. When I say "taken over," I mean that their behavior followed the changes anticipated at very precise frequencies. Waves below 6 cycles per second caused the subjects to become very emotionally upset, and even disrupted bodily functions. At 8.2 cycles, they felt very high, an elevated feeling, as though they had been in masterful meditation learned over a period of years. Eleven to 11.3 cycles induced waves of depressed agitation leading to riotous behavior.

The Neurophone

Dr. Patrick Flanagan is a personal friend of mine. In the early 1960s, as a teenager, Pat was listed as one of the top scientists in the world by *Life* magazine. Among his many inventions was a device he called the neurophone—an electronic instrument that can successfully program suggestions directly through contact with the skin. When he attempted to patent the device, the government demanded that he prove it worked. When he did, the National Security Agency confiscated the neurophone. It took Pat two years of legal battle to get his invention back.

In using the device, you don't hear or see a thing; it is applied to the skin, which Pat claims is the source of special senses. The skin contains more sensors for heat, touch, pain, vibration and electrical fields than any other part of the human anatomy. In one of his recent tests, Pat conducted two identical seminars for a military audience—one seminar one night and one the next night, because the size of the room was not large enough to accommodate all of them at one time. When the first group proved to be very cool and unwilling to respond, Patrick spent the next day making a special tape to play at the second seminar. The tape instructed the audience to be extremely warm and responsive and for their hands to become "tingly." The tape was played through the neurophone, which was connected to a wire he placed along the ceiling of the room. There were no speakers, so no sound could be heard, yet the message was successfully transmitted from that wire directly into the brains of the audience. They were warm and receptive, their hands tingled and they responded, according to programming, in other ways that I cannot mention here.

Television

The more we find out about how human beings work through today's highly advanced technological research, the more we learn to control human beings. And what probably scares me the most is that the medium for takeover is already in place. The *television* set in your living room and bedroom is doing a lot more than just entertaining you.

Before I continue, let me point out something else about an altered state of consciousness. When you go into an altered state, you transfer into right brain which results in the internal release of the body's own opiates—enkephalins and beta-endorphins, chemically almost identical to opium. In other words, it feels good and you want to come back for more.

Recent tests by researcher Herbert Krugman showed that, while viewers were watching TV, right-brain activity outnumbered left-brain activity by a ratio of two to one. Put more simply, the viewers were in an altered state, in trance more often than not. They were getting their beta-endorphin "fix."

To measure attention spans, psychophysiologist Thomas Mulholland of the Veterans Hospital in Bedford, Massachusetts, attached young viewers to an EEG machine that was wired to shut the TV set off whenever the children's brains produced a majority of alpha waves. Although the children were told to concentrate, only a few could keep the set on for more than 30 seconds.

Most viewers are already hypnotized. To deepen the trance is easy. One simple way is to place a blank, black frame every 32 frames in the film that is being projected. This creates a 45 beat per minute pulsation perceived only by the subconscious mind—the ideal pace to generate deep hypnosis.

The commercials or suggestions presented following this alpha-inducing broadcast are much more likely to be accepted by the viewer. The high percentage of the viewing audience that has somnambulistic-depth ability could very well accept the suggestions as commands—as long as those commands did not ask the viewer to do something contrary to his morals, religion or self-preservation.

The medium for takeover is here. By the age of 16, children have spent 10,000 to 15,000 hours watching television—that is more time than they spend in school. In the average home, the TV set is on for six hours and 44 minutes per day—an increase of nine minutes from last year and three times the average rate of increase during the 1970s. It obviously isn't getting better. We are rapidly moving into an alpha-level world—very possibly the Orwellian world of *1984*—placid, glassy-eyed, and responding obediently to instructions.

A research project by Jacob Jacoby, a Purdue University psychologist, found that of 2,700 people tested 90 percent misunderstood even such simple viewing fare as commercials and "Barnaby Jones." Only minutes after watching, the typical viewer missed 23 to 36 percent of the questions about what he or she had seen. Of course they did—they were going in and out of trance! If you go into a deep trance, you must be instructed to remember—otherwise you automatically forget.

I have just touched the tip of the iceberg. When you start to combine subliminal messages behind the music, subliminal visuals projected on the screen, hypnotically produced visual effects, sustained musical beats at a trance-inducing pace—you have extremely effective brainwashing.

Every hour that you spend watching the TV set you become more conditioned. And, in case you thought there was a law against any of these things, guess again. There isn't! There are a lot of powerful people who obviously prefer things exactly the way they are. Maybe they have plans for?

Published in issue 2 of The Dot Connector Magazine
(March-April 2009).

Slave

By Walter C. Vetsch

We have no clue as to the previous uses of this planet. It is claimed the planet has existed over four billion years, however, we have no accurate history of even the last million years. Who knows what civilizations may have used this place—called it "home"—and then moved on, vanished or whatever, and were erased from history with the passage of time. Unfortunately, the present population appears to have been predestined for slavery:

> And God blessed them, and God said unto them, Be fruitful, and multiply, and replenish the earth, and *subdue* it: and have *dominion* over the fish of the sea, and over the fowl of the air, and over every living thing that moveth upon the earth. (Genesis 1:28)

This statement is a command to slaves. Obviously, it has nothing to do with the intent of a true God. The correct command would be something to the effect that man should cooperate with nature, because man and nature were specifically created to be complementary and codependent. This was the belief system of the American Indians and it worked just fine for them. The other "primitive" people who lived alongside them likely had a similar belief system, however, since we killed all of them and they are now extinct, we will never know.

Actually, the "slave commands" in the Christian Bible fall more in line with the philosophy of Zecharia Sitchin. He argues that present man was created by aliens by genetically upgrading orangutans using some of their own (alien) DNA. They were designed to mine and process gold. The gold found on Earth has certain desirable qualities which make it unique as compared to gold on other planets. It is used by advanced civilizations for life extension. Unfortunately, they added enough DNA to upgrade their new creature (man) into Group 1,[18] which made them Spiritually capable. Also, because DNA transfers memories, the latent urge to study the Physical Universe with a desire to return "home" (i.e., the home of their creators) was also transferred. The slaves were to be destroyed at the conclusion of the mission, however, there was some disagreement, and so they were left here on their own when the mission ended and their creators and masters returned to their home planet.

You might also notice that the "creators" are called "sons of God" and their upgraded slaves were so genetically close that they could mate with them and produce offspring ("the sons of God saw the daughters of men that they *were* fair; and they took them wives of all which they chose," Genesis 6:2). However, even though there are many "sons of God" in the Old Testament, there is strangely only one—namely Jesus—in the New Testament who is claimed to be the only "son of God." So, there seems to be a continuity problem here.

Today, the industrialized world faithfully follows the "*subdue*" command. We destroy nature. We wreck the environment. We have so much "*dominion*" over life that we now alter the fundamental codes of life (DNA) to suit our fancy. Eventually, the planet will no longer be able to support any life.

Fully developed Group 1 life forms cannot be enslaved. The two qualities which give them "immunity" from enslavement are commonly called "self-realization" and "God realization". Therefore, to enslave a society of Group 1 beings, you first need to scheme up ways to destroy these qualities. The techniques used to accomplish this fall into the general category of "black magic." Essentially, what you want to accomplish is to break the link between the Soul (which is immortal) and the mind (which is not). Since the mind processes in-

---

18. Groups (classes) of physical bodies are explained in detail in our books *TEXT* (CreateSpace, 2015) and *Playthings of the gods* (CreateSpace, 2015).

formation sort of like a computer, once the link to the Divine is broken, the principle of "garbage in—garbage out" applies. At this stage, the mind can be programmed to accept anything as "truth" and act accordingly. This is the state of mankind today. Now, we will discuss in more detail how this devolution was accomplished.

Use of Propaganda to Destroy Spirituality

Propaganda was the original technique used to Spiritually degrade the general population. It was designed by the priestcraft and continues to this day. The technique involves Spiritually devolving the newborn by programming the parents with unnatural sex instructions designed to bring babies into the world in a Spiritually confused and degraded state.

The Catholics, for example, teach women that they should lie perfectly still and have no emotion or thought of pleasure during sex. Other religions forbid even looking at the girl and require that she be covered with a sheet with a hole in the correct place.

This, of course, is essentially the same as rape. Even Indian Spiritual Masters, who generally oppose abortion, have stated that, in cases of rape, abortion is better than "bringing a beast into the world." This is because sex without love is likely to produce a less than human creature. Of course, this is what the Catholics and others want. They don't want true human beings but rather "smart animals" they can train and control to their liking.

Other Methods to Destroy Spirituality

- POISON THE WATER SUPPLY. People need water to survive, so this is an easy way to make sure a targeted population is affected. This idea is not new. The Romans did it. Recall, the Roman Empire had an elaborate water delivery system. Houses had running water. However, the water supply to the "ordinary" people was delivered through *lead* (Pb) pipes. So, they were being deliberately degraded by lead poisoning. The Roman elite knew lead was poison. Therefore, the water supply to the Roman elite was delivered through clay pipes. Just as today, the ordinary people were clueless and had no idea what was going on. Today, governments poison the water supply with *fluoride*. Fluoride causes what has been described as a "mild lobotomy" and degrades psychic abilities. Just as in Rome, the ordinary people (sheeple) are totally clueless. Obviously, the elite do not drink the same water. Just like the Roman elite, they have access to pure water.

• DUAL USE AGENTS. We use created chemical agents constantly. These chemicals never existed naturally in nature. They exist in everything we use every day. Examples are personal products like shampoo, makeup, deodorants, as well as laundry products and cleaning products. Many of these contain what is known as "aromatic hydrocarbons." These are the things we detect through smell. When we smell them, some of the chemical is getting into our bodies. Since these things are not food or food additives, there is little regulation and essentially no public knowledge of how our bodies are being affected. Many reportedly have mind altering and mind controlling effects similar to the fluoride used to poison our drinking water.

• POISON THE FOOD SUPPLY. In today's "civilized" world, most people are isolated from nature. In cities, the only way to get food is to go to a store and buy processed food. Essentially anything can be added to this "food." Therefore, the government can dope up people with pretty much anything and cover it all up under "national security." The latest scam is to alter the DNA of natural food so that it is unfit for consumption by any living thing. Although many countries have banned this "frankenfood," the U.S. allows it and prohibits people from knowing if the food they buy has been genetically modified.

• ELECTRONIC MIND CONTROL TECHNOLOGIES. The U.S. did not spend thirty years and billions of dollars doing secret mind control experiments under the MKULTRA program for nothing. Specific techniques were perfected, tested, and are in general use today. The government is said to have 85% of the general population under mind control. For some reason, about 15% of the population appears to have some yet unexplained natural immunity and cannot be easily controlled. Therefore, mind control research has never stopped. The code name for the current active project is reportedly MARATHON.

The most common mind control mechanism is *television*. The government freaked out when it was decided to switch to high definition TV. If people lose their daily "fix" of TV propaganda they might start to actually think for themselves which simply cannot be tolerated. So, the government gave away coupons to get special converters to make sure the stream of propaganda would not be interrupted.

Destruction of Family Unit

The family unit is the basic unit of society. Originally, families stayed together and supported and helped one another. Because of this bond, older members were helped by younger members and the youth benefited from the knowledge of the life experiences of the elders who would tell them the truth and prepare them for what lay ahead. Today, this natural arrangement has been effectively destroyed.

The technique used was the tried and proven "divide and conquer" method. By manipulating the economy, moms were forced to get jobs and so could not stay at home. The kids were handed over to daycare centers run by professionals regulated by the state and trained in scientific atheism. So, the kids were alienated from the parents. Some daycare centers secretly used the kids as sex slaves and also for Satanic rituals. Since parents were now literally worked to death just to get enough money to put food on the table, the quality time with their kids was limited. TV programmed the kids with state-controlled propaganda. The elderly were dumped in nursing homes where they were given mind control drugs to turn them into drooling vegetables who could not remember the life they had just lived. Therefore, they could not pass along valuable life experience information to children and grandchildren as had been done in the past. Consequently, the only source of information for the young was state-controlled propaganda through the mandatory state education system and state-controlled TV.

Kids who somehow were able to evade government mind control methods could be taken away by child protective services (CPS) where, in some cases, they were either sold or rented out to the sex slave industry. Additionally, in the U.S., about 100,000 kids are "disappeared" every year. Some are auctioned off as sex slaves. Some are used to harvest organs. Others are used by the Satanists who run our government for sacrifices in occult rituals.

Regression to Animal Existence

We humans like to believe that we are above animals. After all, animals have a miserable existence. From birth, they must constantly fight for survival. If they can't find food or water, they die. If they get sick or hurt, some other animal will kill them and eat them. We claim to have "evolved" to a stage where we are above all this. We claim to respect life and help each other. We claim we care for the sick, injured and less fortunate.

At times, this has been true. However, those times are now ending with the proliferation of predatory capitalism, the social model promoted by the United States which it is determined to export—by force—to every corner of the Earth.

Predatory capitalism returns humankind to the level of the jungle animal. To survive, you must exploit other people and scheme up ways to take away their assets. If you are clever and ruthless enough to crush others, you can become a millionaire or billionaire and be considered a "successful capitalist." However, if you are not a ruthless sociopath, you will be "devoured" just like animals in the jungle. If you are poor, you starve. If you are poor and sick, you are left to die. No one cares. No one is coming to help you. A wild deer with an injured leg probably has a better chance to live than you do. This is the state of the world we created.

Debt Slavery

Debt slavery varies in severity from country to country because of different regulations on usury. Usury is forbidden by the Quran which likely explains why Muslim countries have irreconcilable differences with other countries which love to get rich by loaning out money. So, there is a legal spread on the concept of usury from essentially no tolerance to complete tolerance depending upon where you live.

A documentary focusing on India showed children—5, 6, 7 years old—out in the hot sun (120°F/48.8°C is not uncommon in summer there) making mud bricks. The factory owner was asked, "Why aren't these kids in school?" He replied, "They cannot go to school until the debt is repaid. Until then, they are my property."

You see, in India, debt transfers from parents to children. So, if one of your relatives got, say, a "payday loan" years ago at the standard 5000% annualized interest rate, then all relatives beyond that point would become slaves of the loan holder until it was repaid. Of course, it will never be repaid, so the loan holder legally owns the kids, and their kids, throughout time, forever.

In the United States, a person's debt obligations generally end with physical death and cannot be transferred further. However, laws change and, since laws in the U.S. are made based upon how much money those who want the law are able to pay politicians in bribes, for the right price U.S. citizens could well find themselves in the same condition as the Indian kids at some point down the road.

Lord Rothschild, who lives in London, loves usury. His net worth is estimated to be 500 trillion dollars. Guess how he got it. "Give me control over a country's money, and I care not who makes its laws."

There are only three countries left who do not have a Rothschild family controlled central bank. They are Cuba, North Korea, and Iran. Probably just a coincidence that these are countries with whom United States has "issues."

Entire countries can also be captured and enslaved by these techniques. A good current example is Greece.

The Casino Model

Most people understand that it is impossible to consistently win money by gambling at a casino. As a patron, you always lose eventually. However, the casino owner always wins. This, of course, is because the game is rigged in favor of the house. If you don't want to lose, you can choose not to go into the casino.

However, if the entire world is a big casino (and it is), you cannot choose not to gamble, because you were born in the casino and there is no way to leave. Casino owners—the elite—always win, and casino patrons—the general population—always lose. The technical term for this is "wealth extraction." That is why Lord Rothschild has 500 trillion dollars, and you can't even feed your family. Eventually, the casino owners will own the entire world and the general population will be returned to the life serfs had in the Middle Ages. Barring some kind of revolution, this will be your fate. The system has been engineered to guarantee this.

Since you cannot leave the casino, as an ordinary person, the only way to cut your loses is to gamble as little as possible. This means limiting your participation in establishment society as much as possible. If you can find cooperative people, you can arrange situations where people help one another with life's essential needs as they once did when small groups survived as hunter-gatherers. Money did not exist then and neither did money manipulators. For example, if a group of neighbors agree to form some type of co-op they can buy food in bulk at wholesale prices and then divide it up and share it resulting in considerable savings. You can't totally leave the casino, but you can find creative ways to diminish your rate of "wealth extraction".

Corporate Slavery

Capitalism is simply privatized communism. In classical communism, the state owns everything and everyone works for the state. In capitalism, private corporations own the means of production and, to survive, you must "volunteer" to work for them. When the corporations unite with the central government, as they have in the United States, the system is known as *fascism*.

Corporations are able to enslave people, because they control access to essential goods and services—like food, shelter and medical care—people need to survive. Since people long ago abandoned the hunter-gatherer lifestyle where they were capable surviving on their own, they need some kind of "overlord" and "law giver" to replace the self-sufficiency they once had but have now lost. Out of fear of starvation or illness, they now surrender their freedom to corporations in exchange for a sense of security. Employees of corporations are not technically slaves. They are completely free to walk away at any time. Of course, if they do, they die from starvation or illness. So, they voluntarily submit to a life of slavery.

Kids Broken Through Education System

The education system for the general population is designed to produce obedient slaves. It is not designed to produce free thinking, inquisitive people. It is designed to produce a bunch of "lemmings" who are conditioned to accept whatever is told to them by some authority figure to be correct. They are programmed not to question authority.

To help get the message across that they have no rights, militarized police now patrol schools with attack dogs so the kids will quickly learn to abandon all hope and submit. Kids can be randomly searched without cause, because kids are not considered adults and so have no civil rights. Lately, it has also become popular to allow teachers to carry guns, "just in case." Consequently, after twelve years of this psychological abuse, when they turn eighteen and so theoretically have civil rights, the previous twelve years of experience has taught them to submit to any authority figure without question.

Of course, the children of the elite do not go to public school. They go to very special and very exclusive private schools. Here, they are taught what everyone was once taught. They learn to think independently. They learn to question. They learn to analyze as opposed to just accepting facts as true with no investigation. Additionally, they are taught that they are "exceptional" and that you are not.

Internet of Things

"Internet of things" is the phrase we use to describe the work in progress of linking all electrical and electronic devices to the internet. The new internet protocol, IPv6, provides enough unique numbers to give essentially everything, including people, a unique IP address. Science fiction writers have warned for many years this day would come—the day when computers would control the world and people would be relegated to some sort of lower class or even exterminated by the "intelligent" machines they created. *Colossus: The Forbin Project*, a fiction movie released in 1970, before most people could even imagine the internet, dramatizes this nightmare scenario which could well actually come to pass.

Today, there is an active movement against AI ("artificial intelligence") to raise public awareness that these things do exist—are increasing—and that the decisions made by an "artificial intelligence" may well be to the detriment of real people with real intelligence.

Alien Cooperation and Normalizing

To prepare the Earth for the proposed "New World", the Satanic overlords who run this place have decided to make certain *changes*. Sometimes, the reasons for these changes are not obvious. For example, consider nicotine. You may not recall, but nicotine was the main active ingredient in insecticides for many years. It kills insects dead. Since we developed secret relations with aliens, some of whom are insectoids (advanced insect races), nicotine and, therefore, cigarette smoke is harmful to them. Use of tobacco products has never been permitted in the secret underground cities and installations, because in these protected areas aliens are free to mingle with humans. However, aliens sometimes desire to move about on the surface disguised as humans. This has led to the new movement to have "smoking-free cities" to accommodate these desires.

There are many changes the true nature of which you would probably never guess. Lead paint is a good example. The government uses X-ray satellites to watch people inside of houses and buildings. Lately, local police have been provided with previously classified technologies which include portable X-ray devices to look into people's houses from the outside. Since lead blocks X-rays, it was important to get rid of lead paint. Otherwise these spy devices could not effectively operate.

The most disturbing aspect of the New World is the population limiting initiative. Henry Kissinger reportedly feels that 98% of the people in the world are "useless" and should be killed. The Georgia Guidestones recommend that the population (of slaves) be limited to and maintained at five hundred million. No one involved in this has recommended any percentage below 90%.

This population adjustment event is known among the elite as "The Great Culling." In the United States, the unwanted people are to be exterminated at the FEMA death camps. These slaughter houses are modern and automated. Reportedly, those picked up are to be wrapped in a type of full body straight jacket so that they are straight, stiff, and immobilized. Then they are to be loaded on to a conveyor belt. Beyond this point, the process is automated. The conveyor belt takes the person to an automatic guillotine device where they are beheaded. Then the dead bodies are reportedly to be processed into animal feed. The system is designed to kill people at the rate of sixty per minute, so, apparently, they are quite serious about the 90% figure. The plan is set to be activated as soon as the U.S. President signs the order proclaiming martial law. Hitler would be proud.

The Hive Mind

Human beings are naturally individuals and are therefore capable of unique and independent thought and action. However, not all living creatures have these qualities. Group IV creatures, which include insects, generally operate under a group Soul and do not have individual Souls. They operate under what might be called a "hive mind" in which all individual insects are coordinated by a central command center—the group Soul—so that they function collectively as a single unit. One group of our alien "friends," commonly called "the greys," are insectoids and, although advanced, operate under the same rules which govern our domestic insects.

With the correct persuasion, unfortunately, human beings can be programmed to abandon their individuality and be co-opted into operating under the control of a hive mind. Their individuality is absorbed into the collective. This is the sad state of humanity today.

It is primarily facilitated by technology. By artificially linking individuals with a web of controlled information through television, motion pictures, print media and the internet, it has become possible to cause humanity to adopt coordinated thought patterns and operate under the control of an electronic hive mind coordinated by a central authority. This, effectively, devolves Group I humans to the level of Group IV subhuman creatures.

Independent thought is now considered to be "abnormal." To parrot whatever the mainstream TV news says is considered "normal." To question the party line makes you a "conspiracy theorist." Essential skills are being deleted from the public education system. Kids use calculators instead of learning to do basic math. Teaching handwriting is proposed to be eliminated, because no one uses it any more—everyone types on computers or sends text messages. So, conventional longhand handwriting is considered obsolete. If you believe all this is some type of "plot," you can be labeled "paranoid" and taken away for brainwashing to be "cured."

Mineral Consciousness

When you walk along the ocean shore, the sand below your feet is not alive. It has no consciousness. It has no Soul. It is simply a mineral. However, with clever manipulation, minerals like sand can be configured to have the appearance of consciousness when energized by electricity.

Essentially all of the creature comforts we enjoy today are based upon solid state electronics, and the basic building block of all of these things is silicon or, more plainly stated, sand.

So, with his cleverness, man has created a new state of consciousness—"mineral consciousness"—which has never existed naturally. Mineral consciousness is below all other states of consciousness. However, in today's world, people have come to respect mineral consciousness, depend upon it and, in many cases, consider mineral consciousness to be above human consciousness. The full extent of this craziness can be seen in the desire to abandon human consciousness and descend completely into mineral consciousness.

Since minerals were never alive, they cannot die. So people dream of transferring their human consciousness into mineral consciousness so that they will "live forever." Couples want to create robot copies of their mate so that they can always be together. There is actually a movement, called "Avatar Project," by serious scientists to convert all people to robots so that they can have "everlasting life." People actually believe this crap. Because of scientific atheism, they have totally forgotten that people are actually Souls, and Souls *do have* everlasting life. And, although robots may appear to have everlasting life, they do not have Souls.

Of course, people have forgotten all that. Somehow, in the process of getting addicted to technology, they have totally disregarded all the natural abilities a human body potentially has if you were to devote as much time to developing yourself as you do to developing sophisticated technologies which have no Spiritual merit and function to bind you to the lowest possible state of consciousness.

Thanks for the Memmemmormee?[19]

By Walter H. Bowart (1939–2007)

More than 25 years have passed since I began research into what was then called "brainwashing," a comically euphemistic term invented in the 1950s by CIA propaganda specialist Edward Hunter. It's been 21 years since my book on the subject, *Operation Mind Control*,[20] was published internationally, and five years since it reappeared as the greatly expanded Limited Researcher's Edition, featuring an account of "Lois" that offers a synopsis of the book you hold in your hands.[21] Now it can be told. "Lois" is Susan Ford, whose pseudonym is Brice Taylor. Her book *Thanks for the Memories*, which by all reports is greatly anticipated by an audience better educated than the one I encountered in the 1970s, is now published for all the world to read.

I wrote my book *Operation Mind Control* while living in Arizona, still "a backward state," dominated by Federal funds and jobs and the dissociated and extremely provincial beliefs that come with it. In the 1970s, most of the people I spoke with about what I called generically "mind control" thought I was crazy. Those who were not afraid to express their opinions on the subject believed it to be impossible. They strongly believed they could not be made to do something against their will and without their own knowledge. They believed they had indomitable powers of will, like the CIA-funded psychologist, Timo-

---

19. James Joyce, *Finnigan's Wake*, 1938.
20. Walter H. Bowart, *Operation Mind Control*, Flatland, 1994.
21. The present article is Walter Bowart's foreword to the book: Brice Taylor, *Thanks For The Memories: The Truth Has Set Me Free! The Memoirs of Bob Hope's and Henry Kissinger's Mind-Controlled Slave*. Brice Taylor Trust, 1999.

thy Leary's fellow debater and Watergate burglar, G. Gordon Liddy. They believed, beyond a shadow of a doubt, that they could not be broken, fragmented, and mentally enslaved by any technology, even if it included hypnosis, drugs, electronic brain stimulation or what came to be called biological process control.

My interest in this subject was piqued by a young man, David, I had known all my life. He returned from a four-year tour with the United States Air Force in a confused and deeply tormented state. You could not say that he had a destroyed mind. He suffered from complete amnesia about the past years of service in the USAF, but he was making straight "A's" in premedical courses at a prominent University.

I did not recognize him as he sat, slumped in an overstuffed chair in my living room in 1973. He had undergone a couple of years of treatment with a competent psychiatrist and was finally asked by her, "Do you want to know what this is and how it was created, or do you just want to be able to function?" He decided the functioning was good enough, and his treatment accelerated, taking a wide turn away from the historical events he remembered, which included being a "human tape recorder" and witnessing the most secret negotiations with North Vietnam and with "Royals" of the Arabic persuasion who beheaded a prisoner he had just witnessed being interrogated. The image of this decapitation still haunts him in his dreams.

In 1973, the Rockefeller Commission's Report revealed that CIA Director Richard Helms had supposedly destroyed 153 separate files on a long running, top secret project called MKULTRA, as his last act in office.

In years to come, many of those files were discovered as "misplaced" files. They revealed a long history of criminal activities by individuals who hid behind the National Security Act and ran amok, arrogantly treating citizens of their own country as just so many lab rats.

"I can hypnotize a man—without his knowledge or consent—into committing treason against the United States..." (Dr. George Estabrooks, 1943). This Canadian-born Rhodes Scholar was a hypnosis expert and former professor at Colgate University with long-stand-ing ties to U.S. military and domestic intelligence and to Martin Orne, MD, a master "spy-chiatrist," author of Patty Hearst's "brainwashing" defense, and founding Board member of the False Memory "Spindrome" Foundation (FMSF).

As I was researching the Rockefeller Commission's Report, following anecdotal evidence, putting the pieces together, then writing what turned out to be *Operation Mind Control,* I felt like the villagers in this Sufi tale:

> An elephant had entered a cave near a town in Morocco and had bellowed all night, keeping the whole village awake. Nobody in the town had seen an elephant, nor did anyone know what an elephant looked like.
>
> The villagers held a meeting and four brave people among them volunteered to go into the cave to investigate what was making the strange bellowings.
>
> The first one felt the elephant's trunk and came running out to report a large python was making the noise they heard
>
> The second one felt afoot and came out to report that a palm tree was making the noise. The third one felt the elephant's tail and came out to report that a broom, obviously controlled by a witch, was making the noise.
>
> The fourth villager felt the elephant's ear and came out to report that there was nothing to fear, because a large leaf from a tropical plant was making the noise.
>
> Once they understood there was nothing to fear, the villagers went to sleep that night and didn't hear the elephant snorting and bellowing as he left the cave. Nor did they mention it again.

In those days, shrinks (psychiatrists and psychologists) told me that what I was reporting were the results of a disease called "schizophrenia." The word meant fragmented personality, but in time, schizophrenia turned out to be a familial disease which could be treated and controlled with medication. The stories I was reporting took several years to understand. I eventually discovered that what I was reporting was the real cause of the cryptocracy's trained elephant in the particular cave next to our hometown.

I cannot tell you the experiences Sue Ford reports are accurate to the letter, since I was not a witness to all of them. But, as I revealed in *Operation Mind Control*, I once saw Sue on a Palm Springs golf course in the company of her alleged handler, Bob Hope. At that time I was Editor-in-Chief of *Palm Springs Life* magazine, which had just won the "Maggie" Award for publishing the best city magazine. It was at the Bob Hope Classic that I saw Sue, but I didn't speak to her, as I was busy covering the happenings and celebrities which have graced the magazine since the 1950s. Sue was one of the Bob Hope Classic hostesses, assisting the public and the press in a variety of functions.

My path crossed Sue's again years later, when I was interviewing another survivor of mind control, but I'll spare you those details. Just read my book. I can tell you that Sue Ford believes the story she has written with all her being, and her account as described herein has remained consistent.

Most of her memories conveyed in her book she obtained outside of the therapy setting on the Island of Kauai, while journaling on the beach, since she could not afford a therapist at that time. The perceived safety of the location and the steady sound of the waves in the background provided her with the ability to focus inward, allowing intense flashbacks to recur, including intense memory of her physical sensations during those events (called body memories), all of which she was able to write down in her journals. Sue's journals are amazingly free of mistakes, and that's no small feat since they were written in indelible ink. One gets the impression that Sue simply "downloaded" this material from her inner "multiple personalities," who were desperately wanting to get this information out.

Offering up these truths in these post-False Memory "Spindrome" Foundation days takes courage. The well-funded "foundation," composed of alleged pedophiles and spy-chiatrists (my term for professionals who worked for the CIA in mind control projects over a period of approximately fifty years), has led an effective fight in the courts to establish the fact that a person can easily be made to believe things which are not true. When I asked many of those who would later sit on the FMSF Board if a person could be made to do something against their will and without their knowledge, they denied that it was possible in the mid-seventies.

They have not yet turned their earlier stance completely around. Nor have they taken the next step to offer proof that a person can be made to do something against their will and without their knowledge, but they have gone far enough with their argument that "justice is no longer served by 'eyewitness' accounts." Responding to FMSF lawsuits, the State of California, I'm told, has made new laws which would disqualify the testimony of anyone who has ever confessed to having been hypnotized.

Most lawyers and judges don't understand dissociative disorders, because most "mental health professionals" don't understand them and/or haven't bothered to educate the judicial branch of government. To begin to understand the full range of dissociative disorders, from post-traumatic stress disorder to bipolar disorder to the former multiple personality disorder (MPD, now called DID—dissociative identity disorder), one must confront the National Security State and its military-industrial complex, which created the killers who all too often came home from their service to their country to beat and sexually abuse their wives and children.

One gets the impression today that the majority of both "mental health experts" and judges believe that multiple personality disorder can easily be faked during expert examinations. However, most professionals with experience treating dissociative identity disorder will tell you that it is almost impossible to fake an autonomic response, the kind of response that is used to assess the reality of a dissociated state. Faking an autonomic response would be about as easy as deliberately dilating or contracting your pupils without any change of light stimulus.

On one case the Freedom of Thought Foundation sent me to investigate, the case of Robert Joe Moody, an alleged serial killer with a top secret security clearance in the U.S. Marine Corps, I brought one of the leading experts in the treatment of dissociative identity disorder into the prison conference room. Within minutes this doctor had the killer manifesting four different personalities. When he first switched into the killer personality, the room filled with heat. The doctor told me it was not unusual for a whole variety of physical changes to occur when a multiple switched. The room quickly getting hot from the temperature change of Moody's body when he switched from one personality to the other is a good example of the sort of autonomic response I'm talking about. I'd like to see even the best-trained actor do that on cue!

After the interview with Moody, as we were leaving the prison, the doctor said to me, "Well, what do you want to do? Integrate these personalities, or just let the little nine-year-old personality take the punishment (death by lethal injection) for all the others, just like he has always been doing?"

In the only study of death row inmates in America, roughly 14% tested as being undiagnosed cases of DID. Only a few prisons were used in this study. It focused only on convicted murderers and did not investigate violent criminals who were convicted of assault or crimes less than murder. Other non-capital offenders were omitted. This study clearly showed the ignorance, or prejudice, of the American judicial system, one in which the diagnosis "malingering" is given to people suffering from DID. Malingering is a psychiatric term that means the subject is faking an illness. The poorly trained psychologists and psychiatrists working as court appointed "expert witnesses" don't know how to test nor diagnose dissociative disorders.

The most tragic moment of Moody's story, for most, is when they view the police videotape of the accused killer being read the Miranda Warnings. Here, clearly, is the nine-year-old personality, "Bobby," picking at a scab on his hand, speaking in a halting voice, not understanding who he was, due to amnestic fugue, nor what the words in the Miranda Warnings meant. It was the only time the accused was read his rights. And as you might expect, Bobby wasn't the killer, nor was he even present at the scene of the crime. The killer personality was named XE and was, by all present indications, created during Moody's service in the Marine Corps.

"Mental health professionals" generally overlook the possibility of deliberate programming. Or maybe that's part of the conspiracy against freedom of thought. Many shrinks are themselves unwitting accomplices in this conspiracy. Professional expressions of denial about the access and deliberate programming of dissociated children by agents of National Security States is about as comforting as if they'd told you that the conclusions of the Warren Commission Report were accurate and correct. Even certain members of the International Society for the Study of Dissociative Disorders has put DID in a separate legal category, so that people expressing multiple personalities cannot be found "not guilty by reason of insanity."

Dr. Colin Ross, one of the leading experts on dissociative disorders, expressed the opinion that DID may be the cause of most of the serious problems of our society, such as gangsterism, drive-by shootings, schoolyard assassinations, random acts of terrorism and all the rest of the trauma America has been experiencing over the past few years—an idea not yet examined by criminologists, prison experts, and others who would supposedly protect and serve.

To understand dissociation is to understand the paradigm shift in our culture—from an industrial culture to an information culture. To understand it is to look into the heart of the Dissociated States of America and the Dissociated States of Europe and the Orient.

The seeds of dissociation have been sown throughout history, from our earliest recorded days until the present. You can find evidence of it in the first terrors of the cavemen, in the shamanic practices of most primitive cultures, to the present co-option of severely dissociated people found among the ranks of modem military recruits. A cross section of our society finds its way into military service, and a representational number of them suffer from dissociative disorders. These form a fertile pool for recruitment of programmed personnel.

After you've met a few of them, you realize they have one thing is common—they are highly suggestible. Thus, it is easy to capitalize on the trauma implanted in their child's mind by daddy, uncle, a neighbor or whomever. Once dissociation shows up in the military "entrance tests," they are sorted out for programming. From their ranks are created autonomic assassins, amnestic couriers, and Mata Hari sexpionage agents who've given their involuntary all with no consent form requested.

Who would do such a thing you ask? Read on. Learn about the cryptocracy that has been gradually amassing its power over the human mind since the days when the swastika was forced underground and its armbands torn from the sleeves, but its legacy was not removed from the hearts and minds of those welcomed to America under Operation Paperclip, when Nazi war criminals, posing as scientists, were flown from the front, hidden among those who had spilled their blood fighting fascism.

The value of programming to the cryptocrats is understood when you realize its usefulness in harnessing a slave labor force and covering up crimes. More than one forensic psychiatrist has told me that our criminal justice systems are not prepared to deal with these cases. And it's been that way for quite some time. The litigious actions of the False Memory "Spindrome" Foundation have done further damage to justice by successfully obfuscating the realities of dissociative disorders and by blaming its cause on the treatments of incompetent "mental health professionals."

Whether a victim of DID, trained and conditioned and honed for government use, claims they have been raised in a Satanic cult, or a secret society, or been abducted by aliens—matters not at all. For eons of time, throughout the entire history of mankind (as far as we know) war and trauma have created this evil, which is multigenerational, passed down the family tree from parent to child in an unbroken chain. The flavor of the torture matters not—it is nonetheless torture.

The style of programming matters not—it is nonetheless programming. Usually the women are turned into slaves of one kind or another; the men are turned into killers or handlers. Regardless of the content of their story, the professional can only take it at face value, support the client, use it as a metaphor if nothing else, and try one technique after another until they get the results they are seeking, reintegration and eventual recovery.

After spending the past five years studying programmed killers, it is refreshing to turn once again to Sue Ford's case. Most of us cannot keep from wincing at her vivid descriptions in certain parts. Others similarly victimized have experienced tortures so terrible (literally unspeakable) that they might think Sue had a "privileged" time of it. Though, Sue was used at a very "high level" in such ways that required her physical preservation. Many survivors, it would appear, are generally too incapacitated to write their own story and too destitute or crippled to achieve sufficient recovery.

Sue's story, truly a spy-chiatrist's "nightmare come true," is like a fascinating, multifaceted gemstone washed up on a white, sandy Hawaiian beach after having battled typhoons, rip tides and the treacherous forces of man and nature. It is the story of a survivor who truly has emerged as a Victor against all odds.

We must salute Sue. She has preceded the therapeutic community's understanding of dissociation and reintegration in the context of mind control. She's been a teacher as well as a patient, and has inspired many of those who are leading the way toward real healing, not just a drugging of symptoms as is too commonly found to be the "mental health" cure for MPD/DID. Through her valiant recovery from trauma-based mind control, Sue has paved the way for other survivors to follow.

Project Monarch:
Nazi Mind Control

By Ron Patton

Amidst the subtle cerebral circumvention of the gullible populace, through a multitude of manipulated mediums, lies one of the most diabolical atrocities perpetrated upon a segment of the human race; a form of systematic mind control which has permeated every aspect of society for over fifty years. To objectively ascertain the following, one may need to re-examine preconceived ideologies relating to the dualistic nature of mankind. Resolving the philosophical question of whether we are inherently good or inherently evil is tantamount in shaping our perception of reality; specifically, the spiritual variable within the equation of life. This exposition is substantiated by declassified U.S. government documents, individuals formerly connected to the U.S. intelligence communities, historical writings, researchers knowledgeable in mind control, publications from mental health practitioners, and interviews taken from survivors unwittingly subjected to a highly complex form of trauma-based mind control known as MONARCH programming. A word of caution for survivors of intensively systematic mind control and/or some form of ritualized abuse: *There are numerous "triggers" in this article.* It is therefore recommended not to read it unless appropriate support systems are in place or if you have a thoroughly reintegrated personality.

A Brief History of Control

The Mystery Religions of ancient Egypt, Greece, India and Babylon helped lay the foundation for occultism, meaning "hidden knowledge." One of the earliest writings giving reference to occultism is the Egyptian Book of the Dead, a compilation of rituals explicitly describing methods of torture and intimidation (to create trauma), the use of potions (drugs) and the casting of spells (hypnotism), ultimately resulting in the total enslavement of the initiate.[22] These have been the main ingredients for a part of occultism known as Satanism, throughout the ages. During the 13th century, the Roman Catholic church increased and solidified its dominion throughout Europe with the infamous Inquisition. Satanism survived this period of persecution, deeply entrenching itself under the veil of various esoteric groups.

In 1776, a Bavarian Jesuit by the name of Adam Weishaupt was commissioned by the House of Rothschild to centralize the power base of the Mystery Religions into what is commonly known as the Illuminati, meaning "Enlightened Ones." This was an amalgamation of powerful occult bloodlines, elite secret societies and influential masonic fraternities, with the desire to construct the framework for a "New World Order." The outward goal of this Utopia was to bring forth universal happiness to the human race. However, their underlying intention was to gradually increase control over the masses, thus becoming masters of the planet.

The Anglo Alliance

By the 19th century, Great Britain and Germany were recognized as the primary geographic areas of Illuminati control. It then should be of little surprise to know the first work in behavioral science research was established in England in 1882, while much of the early medical and psychiatric techniques involved in mind control were pioneered at the Kaiser Wilhelm Institute in Germany. The Tavistock Institute of Human Relations was set up in London in 1921 to study the "breaking point" of humans. Kurt Lewin, a German psychologist, became the director of the Tavistock Institute in 1932, about the same time Nazi Germany was increasing its research into neuropsychology, parapsychology and multigenerational occultism.

---

22. David L. Carrico. *The Egyptian-Masonic-Satanic Connection.* Self Published, 1992.

Interestingly, a progressive exchange of scientific ideas was taking place between England and Germany, most notably in the field of eugenics—the movement devoted to "improving" the human species through the control of hereditary factors in mating. The nefariously enigmatic union between the two countries was bonded, partly through the Order of the Golden Dawn, a secret society, which consisted of many high ranking officials in the Nazi party and British aristocracy. Top SS Nazi officer Heinrich Himmler was in charge of a scientific project called Lebersborn, which included selective breeding and adoption of children, a peculiarly large number of twins among them.[23] The purpose of the program was to create a super-race (Aryans) who would have total allegiance to the cause of the Third Reich (New World Order).

Much of the preliminary experimentation concerning genetic engineering and behavior modification was conducted by Dr. Josef Mengele at Auschwitz, where he coldly analyzed the effects of trauma-bonding, eye-coloring and "twinning" upon his victims. Beside the insidious surgical experimentation performed at the concentration camp, some of the children were subjected to massive amounts of electroshock. Sadly, many of them did not survive the brutality.

Concurrently, brainwashing was carried out on inmates at Dachau, who were placed under hypnosis and given the hallucinogenic drug mescaline. During the war, parallel behavioral research was led by Dr. George Estabrooks of Colgate University. His involvement with the Army, CID, FBI and other agencies remains shrouded in secrecy. However, Estabrooks would occasionally "slip" and discuss his work involving the creation of hypno-programmed couriers and hypnotically-induced split personalities.[24]

After WWII, the U.S. Department of Defense secretly imported many of the top German Nazi and Italian fascist scientists and spies into the United States via South America and the Vatican. The code

---

23. Walter H. Bowart. *Operation Mind Control.* Flatland Editions, 1994, p. 216.
24. Martin Cannon. Mind Control and the American Government. Prevailing Winds Research, 1994, p. 19.

name for this operation was Operation Paperclip.[25] One of the more prominent finds for the U.S. was German General Reinhard Gehlen. Hitler's Chief of Intelligence against Russia. Upon arriving in Washington, D.C., in 1945, Gehlen met extensively with President Truman, General William "Wild Bill" Donovan, Director of the Office of Strategic Services (OSS) and Allen Dulles, who would later become the stalwart head of the CIA. The objective of their brain-storming sessions was to reorganize the nominal American intelligence operation, transforming it into a highly-efficient covert organization. The culmination of their efforts produced the Central Intelligence Group in 1946, renamed the Central Intelligence Agency in 1947.

Reinhard Gehlen also had profound influence in helping to create the National Security Council, from which the National Security Act of 1947 was derived. This particular piece of legislation was implemented to protect an unconscionable number of illegal government activities, including clandestine mind control programs.

The Evolution of Project MKULTRA

With the CIA and National Security Council firmly established, the first in a series of covert brainwashing programs was initiated by the Navy in the fall of 1947. Project CHATTER was developed in response to the Soviet's "successes" through the use of "truth drugs." This rationale, however, was simply a cover story if the program were to be exposed. The research focused on the identification and testing of such drugs for use in interrogations and the recruitment of agents.[26] The project was officially terminated in 1953.

The CIA decided to expand their efforts in the area of behavior modification with the advent of Project BLUEBIRD, approved by director Allen Dulles in 1950. Its objectives were to: 1) discover a means of conditioning personnel to prevent unauthorized extraction of information from them by known means; 2) investigate the possibility of control of an individual by application of special interrogation

---

25. Linda Hunt. *Secret Agenda*. St. Martin's Press, 1991.
26. Final Report of the Select Committee to Study Governmental Operations. U.S. Senate, April 1976, p. 387.

techniques; 3) investigate memory enhancement, and 4) establish defensive means for preventing hostile control of agency personnel.

In August 1951, Project BLUEBIRD was renamed Project ARTICHOKE, which evaluated offensive uses of interrogation techniques, including hypnosis and drugs. The program ceased in 1956.

Three years prior to the halt of Project ARTICHOKE, Project MKULTRA came into existence on April 13, 1953, along the lines proposed by Richard Helms, Deputy Director of Central Intelligence (DDCI), with the rationale of establishing a "special funding mechanism of extreme sensitivity."[27]

The hypothetical etymology of "MK" may possibly stand for "Mind Kontrolle." (The obvious translation of the German word "Kontrolle" into English is "control."[28]) A host of German doctors, procured from the post-war Nazi talent pool, were an invaluable asset toward the development of MKULTRA. The correlation between the concentration camp experiments and the numerous subprojects of MKULTRA are clearly evident. The various avenues used to control human behavior under MKULTRA included radiation, electroshock, psychology, psychiatry, sociology, anthropology, graphology, harassment substances and paramilitary devices and materials, "LSD" being the most widely dispensed "material." A special procedure, designated MKDELTA, was established to govern the use of MKULTRA abroad. MKULTRA/DELTA materials were used for harassment, discrediting, or disabling purposes.[29]

Of the 149 subprojects under the umbrella of MKULTRA having been identified, Project MONARCH, officially begun by the U.S. Army in the early 1960s (although unofficially implemented much earlier), appears to be the most prominent and is still classified as top secret for "national security" reasons.[30] MONARCH may have culminated from MKSEARCH subprojects, such as operation SPELLBINDER, which

27. *Ibid*, p. 390.
28. John Marks. *The Search for the Manchurian Candidate*. Times Books, 1979, pp. 60-61.
29. Final Report of the Select Committee to Study Governmental Operations. U.S. Senate, April 1976, p. 391.
30. Mark Phillips and Cathy O'Brien, Project Monarch, 1993.

was set up to create "sleeper" assassins (i e., "Manchurian candidates") who could be activated upon receiving a key word or phrase while in a post-hypnotic trance. Operation OFTEN, a study which attempted to harness the power of occult forces, was possibly one of several cover programs to hide the insidious reality of Project MONARCH.

Definition and Description

The name MONARCH is not necessarily defined within the context of royal nobility, but rather refers to the monarch butterfly. When a person is undergoing trauma induced by electroshock, a feeling of lightheadedness is evidenced; as if one is floating or fluttering like a butterfly. There is also a symbolic representation pertaining to the transformation, or metamorphosis, of this beautiful insect—from a caterpillar to a cocoon (dormancy, inactivity) and then to a butterfly (new creation), which will return to its point of origin. Such is the migratory pattern that makes this species unique.

Occult symbolism may give additional insight into the true meaning. Psyche is the word for both "soul" and "butterfly" coming from the belief that human souls become butterflies while searching for a new reincarnation.[31]

Some ancient mystical groups, such as the Gnostics, saw the butterfly as a symbol of corrupt flesh. The "Angel of Death" (remember Mengele?) in Gnostic art works was portrayed crushing the butterfly.[32] A marionette is a puppet that is attached to strings and is controlled by the puppet master, hence MONARCH programming is also referred to as the "marionette syndrome." "Imperial conditioning" is another term used, while some mental health therapists know it as "conditioned stimulus response sequences."

Project MONARCH could be best described as a form of structured dissociation and occult integration in order to compartmentalize the mind into multiple personalities within a systematic framework. During this process, a Satanic ritual, usually including Cabalistic mys-

31. Barbara G. Walker. *The Woman's Dictionary of Symbols and Sacred Objects.* HarperCollins, 1988.

32. Marshall Cavendish. *Man, Myth and Magic.* 1995.

ticism, is performed with the purpose of attaching a particular demon or group of demons to the corresponding alter(s). Of course,
most skeptics would view this as simply a means to enhance trauma
within the victim, negating any irrational belief that demonic possession actually occurs.

Alters and Triggers

Another way of examining this convoluted victimization of body and
soul is by looking at it as a complex computer program. A file (alter)
is created through trauma, repetition, and reinforcement. In order to
activate (trigger) the file, a specific access code or password (cue or
command) is required. The victim/survivor is called a "slave" by the
programmer/handler, who in turn is perceived as "master" or "god."
About 75% are female, since they possess a higher tolerance for pain
and tend to dissociate easier than males. Subjects are used mainly
for cover operations, prostitution and pornography; involvement in
the entertainment industry is notable. A former military officer connected to the DIA, told this writer, "In the 'big picture' these people
[MONARCH victims] are in all walks of life, from the bum on the street
to the white-collar guy." In corroboration, a retired CIA agent vaguely
discussed the use of such personnel to be used as "plants" or "chame-
leons" for the purpose of infiltrating a designated group, gathering
information and/or injecting an ulterior agenda.

There are an inordinate amount of alters in the victim/survivor
with numerous backup programs, mirrors and shadows. A division
of light-side (good) and dark-side (bad) alters are interwoven in the
mind and rotate on an axis.

One of the main internal structures (of which there are many)
within the system is shaped like a double-helix consisting of seven
levels. Each system has an internal programmer which oversees the
"gatekeeper" (demon?) who grant or deny entry into the different
rooms. A few of the internal images predominately seen by victims/
survivors are trees, the Cabalistic "Tree of Life," with adjoining root
systems, infinity loops, ancient symbols and letters, spider webs, mirrors or glass shattering, masks, castles, mazes, demons/monsters/

81

aliens, sea shells, butterflies, snakes, ribbons, bows, flowers, hour-glasses, clocks, robots, chain-of-command diagrams and/or schematics of computer circuitry boards.

Bloodlines and Twinning

A majority of the victims/survivors come from multigenerational Satanic families (bloodlines) and are ostensibly programmed "to fill their destiny as the chosen ones or chosen generations" (a term coined by Mengele at Auschwitz). Some are adopted out to families of similar origin. Others used in this neurological nightmare are deemed as the "expendable ones" (non-bloodliners), usually coming from orphanages, foster care homes, or incestuous families with a long history of pedophilia. There also appears to be a pattern of family members affiliated with government or military intelligence agencies.

Many of the abused come from families who use Catholicism, Mormonism, or charismatic Christianity as a "front" for their abominable activities (though members of other religious groups are also involved.)

Victims/survivors generally respond more readily to a rigid religious (dogmatic, legalistic) hierarchical structure, because it parallels their base programming. Authority usually goes unchallenged, as their will has been usurped through subjective and command-oriented conditioning.

Physical identification characteristics of victims/survivors often include multiple electrical prod scars and/or resultant moles on their skin. A few may have had various parts of their bodies mutilated by knives, branding irons, or needles. Butterfly or occult tattoos are also common. Generally, bloodliners are less likely to have the subsequent markings, as their skin is to "remain pure and unblemished."

The ultimate purpose of the sophisticated manipulation of these individuals may sound unrealistic, depending upon our interpretive understanding of the physical and spiritual realms. The deepest and darkest alters within bloodliners are purported to be dormant until the "antichrist" is revealed. These "New World Order" alters supposedly contain callback orders and instructions to train and/or initiate a large influx of people (possibly clones or "soulless ones"), thereby stimulating social control programs into the new millennium.

Non-biological "twinning" is yet another bizarre feature observed within MONARCH programming. For instance, two young nonrelated children would be ceremoniously initiated in a magical "soul-bonding" ritual so they might be "inseparably paired for eternity" (possibly another Mengele connection). They essentially share two halves of the programmed information, making them interdependent upon one another. Paranormal phenomena such as astral projection, telepathy, ESP, etc., appear to be more pronounced between those who have undergone this process.

Levels of MONARCH Programming[33]

- ALPHA. Regarded as "general" or regular programming within the base control personality; characterized by extremely pronounced memory retention, along with substantially increased physical strength and visual acuity. Alpha programming is accomplished through deliberately subdividing the victims personality, which, in essence, causes a left brain—right brain division, allowing for a programmed union of L and R through neuron pathway stimulation.

- BETA. Referred to as "sexual" programming. This programming eliminates all learned moral convictions and stimulates the primitive sexual instinct, devoid of inhibitions. "Cat" alters may come out at this level.

- DELTA. This is known as "killer" programming, originally developed for training special agents or elite soldiers (i.e., Delta Force, First Earth Battalion, Mossad, etc.) in covert operations. Optimal adrenal output and controlled aggression is evident. Subjects are devoid of fear; very systematic in carrying out their assignment. Self-destruct or suicide instructions are layered in at this level.

- THETA considered to be the "psychic" programming. Bloodliners (those coming from multigenerational Satanic families) were

---

33. Dr. Corydon Hammond. The Greenbaum Speech. 1992; Mark Phillips and Cathy O'Brien. Project Monarch Programming Definitions. 1993.

determined to exhibit a greater propensity for having telepathic abilities than did non-bloodliners. Due to its evident limitations, however, various forms of electronic mind control systems were developed and introduced, namely, biomedical human telemetry devices (brain implants), directed energy lasers using microwaves and/or electromagnetics. It is reported these are used in conjunction with highly-advanced computers and sophisticated satellite tracking systems.

- OMEGA. A "self-destruct" form of programming, also known as "Code Green." The corresponding behaviors include suicidal tendencies and/or self-mutilation. This program is generally activated when the victim/survivor begins therapy or interrogation and too much memory is being recovered.
- GAMMA. Another form of system protection is through "deception" programming, which elicits misinformation and misdirection. This level is intertwined with demonology and tends to regenerate itself at a later time if inappropriately deactivated.

Method and Components

The initial process begins with creating dissociation within the subject, usually occurring from the time of birth to about six years. This is primarily achieved through the use of electroshock (ECT) and is at times performed even when the child is in the mother's womb. Due to the severe trauma induced through ECT, sexual abuse and other methods, the mind splits off into alternate personalities from the core. Formerly referred to as multiple personality disorder (MPD), it is presently recognized as dissociative identity disorder (DID) and is the basis for MONARCH programming. Further conditioning of the victim's mind is enhanced through hypnotism, double-bind coercion, pleasure/pain reversals, food, water, sleep and sensory deprivation, along with various drugs which alter certain cerebral functions.

The next stage is to embed and compress detailed commands or messages within the specified alter. This is achieved through the use of hi-tech headsets in conjunction with computer-driven generators which emit inaudible sound waves or harmonics that affect the RNA covering of neuron pathways to the subconscious and unconscious mind. "Virtual reality" optical devices are sometimes used simultaneously with the harmonic generators projecting pulsating colored lights, subliminals, and split-screen visuals. High voltage electroshock is then used for memory dissolution.

Programming is updated periodically and reinforced through visual, auditory and written mediums. Some of the first programming themes included the *Wizard of Oz* and *Alice in Wonderland*, both heavily saturated with occult symbolism. Many of the recent Disney movies and cartoons are used in a two-fold manner: desensitizing the majority of the population, using subliminals and neuro-linguistic programming, and deliberately constructing specific triggers and keys for base programming of highly-impressionable MONARCH children.

A prime example of how subliminal programming works is by looking at the recent Disney cinematic sensation *Pochahontas*, curiously billed as their "33rd" (highest degree in Scottish Rite Freemasonry) animated movie. In the movie, Grandmother Willow is a mystical 400-year-old tree who counsels the motherless Pochahontas to listen to her heart and help her realize all the answers lie within. Grandmother Willow is constantly talking in "doublespeak" and using "reversals," e.g., "Sometimes the right path is not the easiest one," the esoteric derivative being: the left path (the path that leads to destruction) is the easiest one. In Illuminati structured MPD systems, the willow tree represents the occult powers of Druidism. The intrinsic imagery of the tree's branches, leaves and root systems are very significant, as some of the dark spiritual proper ties associated with the "willow tree programming" are: 1) the branches are used to whip victims in rituals for "cleansing" purposes; 2) a willow tree can endure severe weather disturbances (e.g., storms) and is known for it's pliability or flexibility; victims/survivors of the programming describe the willow's branches wrapping around them, with no hope of escape; 3) the deep root system of the willow tree makes the victim/survivor feel as if they are falling deeper and deeper into an abyss while in a hypnotic trance.

Music plays an instrumental role in programming through combinations of variable tones, rhythms, and words. Frightmeister Stephen King's numerous novels and subsequent movies are purported by credible sources to be used for such villainous purposes. One of his latest books, *Insomnia*, features a picture of King with the trigger phrase, "WE NEVER SLEEP" (indicative of someone with MPD/DID), below an all-seeing eye.

A partial list of other mediums used to reinforce base programming are: *Pinocchio, Sleeping Beauty, Snow White, Beauty and the Beast, Aladdin, The Little Mermaid, The Lion King, E.T., Star Wars, Ghostbusters, Trancers II, Batman, Bewitched, Fantasy Island, ReBoot, Tiny Toons, DuckTales, The Dead Sea Scrolls,* and *The Tall Book of Make-Believe*. A few movies which depict or portray some aspect of MONARCH programming are *Hellraiser III, Raising Cain, Labyrinth, Telefon, Johnny Mnemonic, Point of No Return, The Lawnmower Man,* and *Closet Land*.

Programmers and Places

It's difficult to figure out who the original programmer of this Satanic project was, due to the substantial amount of disinformation and cross-contamination propagated by the "powers that be." The two that went by the color-coded name of Dr. Green are a Jewish doctor named Dr. Gruenbaum, who supposedly collaborated with the Nazis during WWII, and Dr. Josef Mengele, whose trademark of cold-blooded and calculated brutality has not only scarred the souls of survivors from Auschwitz, but also a countless number of people throughout the world. Mengele's direct involvement at the infamous Auschwitz concentration camp was suspiciously downplayed during the Nuremberg Trials, and consequently no intensified effort by the U.S. and it's allies was directed toward his capture.[34] As a means to confuse serious investigators as to his whereabouts, U.S. officials would report Mengele being a non-threatening, recluse in Paraguay or Brazil, or that he was simply dead (the "Angel of Death" miraculously must have come back to life at least five different times).

---

34. Gerald L. Posner. *Mengele: The Complete Story.* McGraw-Hill, 1986.

His unprecedented research at the expense of thousands of lives undoubtedly was a significant bonus to u.s. interests, Besides using the pseudonym of Dr. Green, survivors knew him as Väterchen ("daddy"), Schöner Josef ("beautiful Joseph"), David, and Fairchild. A gracefully handsome man of slight stature, Mengele would disarm people with his gentle demeanor, while at other times, he would explode into violent rages.[35] Other characteristics remembered by survivors were the cadence of his shiny black boots as he paced back and forth and his "I love you, I love you not" daisy game. When he pulled off the last daisy petal, he would maliciously torture and kill a small child in front of the other child he was programming. Distraught survivors also recalled being thrown naked into cages with monkeys who were trained to viciously abuse them. Evidently, Mengele enjoyed reducing people to the level of animals. He also would purposely restrain his victims from crying, screaming or showing any excessive emotion.

Dr. D. Ewen Cameron, also known as Dr. White, was the former head of the Canadian, American and World Psychiatric Associations. Because of Cameron's extensive experience and credentials, the CIA's Allen Dulles funneled millions of dollars throughout organizations like the society for the Investigation of Human Ecology, which Cameron ruthlessly presided over. Experimentations were conducted at several locations in Montreal, mostly at McGill University, St. Mary's Hospital and Allan Memorial Institute.

Besides the conventional methods of psychiatric tyranny, such as electroshock drug injections and lobotomies, Cameron conceived the technique of "psychic driving," wherein unsuspecting patients were kept in a drug-induced coma for several weeks and administered a regimen of electroshocks while electronic helmets were strapped to their heads and repetitive auditory messages were transmitted at variable speeds.[36]

35. Lucette Matalon Lagnado. *Dr. Josef Mengele and the Untold Story of the Twins of Auschwitz.* Morrow, 1991.
36. Gordon Thomas. *Journey Into Madness: The Story of Secret CIA Mind Control and Medical Abuse.* Bantam Books, 1989.

Many of those exploited were abused children which had been run through the Roman Catholic orphanage system. Not surprisingly, Dr. Cameron has been conveniently left out of most psychiatric journals. This may have been, in fact, largely due to Project MKULTRA being publicly exposed in 1970 through lawsuits filed by Canadian survivors and their families. The CIA and Canadian government settled out of court so as not to be required to officially admit to any wrongdoing.

A former U.S. Army Lt. Col. in the DIA's Psychological Warfare Division, Michael Aquino, is the latest in a line of alleged government-sponsored sadists. Aquino, an eccentric genius, founded the Temple of Set, an offshoot of Anton LaVey's Church of Satan. His obsession with Nazi pagan rituals and his hypnotic manipulation of people made him an ideal candidate for the position of "Master Programmer." Aquino was connected with the U.S. Army's Presidio base day care scandal, in which he was accused of child molestation. Much to the dismay of the victims' parents, all charges were dismissed. Code-named "Malcolm," Aquino developed training tapes on how to create a MONARCH slave and worked as a liaison between government-military intelligence and various criminal organizations and occult groups in the distribution of MONARCH slaves.[37]

Heinrich Mueller was another important programmer who went under the code names "Dr. Blue" or "Gog." He apparently has two sons who have carried on the trade. The original "Dr. Black" was apparently Leo Wheeler, the nephew of deceased General Earle G. Wheeler, who was the commander of the Joint Chiefs of Staffs during the Vietnam War. Wheeler's protégé, E. Hummel, is active in the Northwest, along with W. Bowers (from the Rothschild bloodline). Other alleged master mind manipulators, past and present, are: Dr. Sydney Gottlieb, Lt. Col. John Alexander, Richard Dabney Anderson (USN), Dr. James Monroe, Dr. John Lilly, Lt. Comdr. Thomas Narut, Dr. William Jennings Bryan, Dr. Bernard L. Diamond, Dr. Martin T. Orne, Dr. Louis J. West, Dr. Robert J. Lifton, Dr. Harris Isbel, and Col. Wilson Green.

---

37. Cathy O'Brien and Mark Phillips. *Trance-Formation of America.* 1995.

In order to keep MKULTRA from being easily detected, the CIA segmented its subprojects into specialized fields of research and development at universities, prisons, private laboratories and hospitals. Of course, they were rewarded generously with government grants and miscellaneous funding.

The names and locations of some of the major institutions involved in MONARCH programming experimentation were/are: Cornell, Duke, Princeton, UCLA, University of Rochester, MIT, Georgetown University Hospital, Maimonides Medical Center, St. Elizabeth's Hospital (Washington, D.C.), Bell Laboratories, Stanford Research Institute, Westinghouse Friendship Laboratories, General Electric, ARCO, and Manking Research Unlimited, The "final product" was/is usually created on military installations and bases, where maximum security is required. Referred to as (re)programming centers or near-death trauma centers, the most heavily identified are: China Lake Naval Weapons Center, The Presidio, Ft. Dietrick, Ft. Campbell, Ft. Lewis, Ft. Hood, Redstone Arsenal, Offutt AFB, Patrick AFB, McClellan AFB, MacGill AFB, Kirkland AFB, Nellis AFB, Homestead AFB, Grissom AFB, Maxwell AFB, and Tinker AFB. Other places recognized as major programming sites are Langley Research Center, Los Alamos National Laboratories, Tavistock Institute, and areas in or by Mt. Shasta, CA, Lampe, MO, and Las Vegas, NV.

Notable Names

One of the first documented cases of a MONARCH secret agent was that of the voluptuous 1940s model Candy Jones. The book, *The Control of Candy Jones* (Playboy Press), portrays her 12 years of intrigue and suspense as a spy for the CIA. Jones, whose birth name is Jessica Wilcox, apparently fit the physiological profile as to be one of the initial experiments or human guinea pigs under the government's "scientific" project MKULTRA.

The most publicized case of MONARCH monomania has surfaced through the book *Trance-Formation of America: The True Life Story of a CIA Slave,* by Cathy O'Brien. On the back cover, it emphatically states: "Cathy O'Brien is the only vocal and recovered survivor of the Central Intelligence Agency's MKULTRA Project MONARCH mind control operation." This documented autobiography contains compelling accounts of O'Brien's years of unrelenting incest and eventual introduction into Project MONARCH by her perverted father. Along with co-author Mark Phillips, her rescuer and deprogrammer, Cathy covers an almost unbelievable array of conspiratorial crime: forced prostitution (white slavery) with those in the upper echelons of world politics, covert assignments as a "drug mule" and courier, and the country-and-western music industry's relationship with illegal CIA activities.

Paul Bonacci, a courageous survivor who endured almost two decades of degradation under Project MONARCH, has disclosed strong corroborating evidence of widescale crimes and corruption from the municipal/state level all the way up to the White House.[38] He has testified about sexually-abused males selected from Boy's Town in Nebraska and taken to nearby Offut AFB, where he says they were subjected to intense MONARCH programming, directed mainly by Commander Bill Plemmons and former Lt. Col. Michael Aquino.[39] After thoroughly tormenting the young boys into mindless oblivion, they were used (along with girls) for pornography and prostitution with several of the nation's political and economic power brokers.

Bonacci recalled being transported from the Air Force base via cargo planes to McClelland AFB in California. Along with other unfortunate adolescents and teenagers, he was driven to the elite retreat, Bohemian Grove. The perpetrators took full advantage of these innocent victims, committing unthinkable perversions in order to satisfy their deviant lusts. Some victims were apparently murdered, further traumatizing already terrified and broken children. An unsuitable actress of marginal talent (now deceased), a morally-corrupt TV evangelist, a heralded former Green Beret officer, and a popular country-and-western singer are a few others likely having suc-

---

38. John DeCamp. *The Franklin Cover-Up, Child Abuse, Satanism and Murder in Nebraska.* AWT Inc., 1992.

39. Anton Chaitkin, "Franklin Witnesses Implicate FBI and U.S. Elites in Torture and Murder of Children." *The New Federalist*, 1993.

cumbed to MONARCH madness. Lee Harvey Oswald, Sirhan Sirhan, Charlie Manson, John Hinckley, Jr., Mark Chapman, David Koresh, Tim McVeigh, and John Salvi are some notable names of infamy, strongly suspected of being pawns who were spawned by MKULTRA.

Deprogrammers and Exposers

Dr. Corydon Hammond, a psychologist from the University of Utah, delivered a stunning lecture, entitled "Hypnosis in MPD: Ritual Abuse," at the Fourth Annual Eastern Regional Conference on Abuse and Multiple Personality, June 25, 1992, in Alexandria, Virginia. He essentially confirmed the suspicions of the attentive crowd of mental health professionals, wherein a certain percentage of their clients had undergone mind control programming in an intensively systematic manner. Hammond alluded to the Nazi connection, military and CIA mind control research, Greek letter and color programming, and specifically mentioned the MONARCH Project in relation to a form of operative conditioning.

Shortly after his groundbreaking speech, he received death threats. Not wanting to jeopardize the safety of his family, Dr. Hammond stopped disseminating any follow-up information, until recently. Mark Phillips, a former electronics subcontractor for the Department of Defense, was privy to some of the top secret mind control activities perpetrated by the U.S. government. His inquisitive demeanor, strong conscience and heartfelt concern for Cathy O'Brien, a "Presidential Model" under Project MONARCH, prompted him to reveal the inner-workings of this grand deception beginning about 1991. As the story goes, he helped Ms. O'Brien escape from her captors and was able to deprogram her in about a year's time in Alaska. The controversial Phillips has his share of critics who are skeptical of the veracity of his claims. New Orleans therapist Valerie Wolf introduced two of her patients before the President's Committee on Human Radiation Experiments on March 15, 1995, in Washington, D.C. The astonishing testimony made by these two brave women included accounts of German doctors, torture, drugs, electroshock, hypnosis and rape, besides being exposed to an undetermined amount of radiation. Both

Wolf and her patients stated they recovered the memories of this CIA program without regression or hypnosis techniques.[40] Wolf presently devotes much of her time to counseling such survivors.

A former labor attorney for Atlantic Richfield Co., David E. Rosenbaum, conducted a nine-year investigation (1983–1992) concerning allegations of physical torture and coercive conditioning of numerous employees at an ARCO plant in Monaca, PA.[41] His clients, Jerry L. Dotey and Ann White, were victims of apparent radiation exposure; but as Mr. Rosenbaum probed deeper in the subsequent interview sessions, a "Pandora's Box" was unveiled. His most astonishing conclusion was that Jerry Dotey and Ann White were likely the offspring of Adolf Hitler, based in part on the uncanny resemblance from photos (facial features, bone structure and size were taken into consideration). Rosenbaum also states, "They both exhibit feelings and experiences that indicate they are twins." Dotey and White were allegedly subjected to torture of many kinds while under drug-induced hypnosis, with each one undergoing at least three training techniques by plant physicians. Each victim was trained to enter into a hypnotic state upon the occurrence of specific stimuli, usually involving a "cue" word or phrase and trained to "remember to forget" what transpired in the hypnotic state. They were repeatedly subjected to identical stimulus-response sequence, to produce nearly automatic reactions to the particular status. MKULTRA veteran, Dr. Bernard Diamond, Dr. Martin Orne and Dr. Josef Mengele regularly visited the ARCO plant, according to Rosenbaum. The special conditioning of Dotey and White was intended for the artificial creation of dual German personalities. Rosenbaum, who is Jewish, has maintained a deep friendship with the two, despite the seemingly precarious circumstances. Other renowned therapists involved in deprogramming are Cynthia Byrtus, Pamela Monday, Steve Ogilvie, Bennett Braun, Jerry Mungadze, and Colin Ross. Journalists who have

---

40. Jon Rappoport. "CIA Experiments with Mind Control on Children." *Perceptions Magazine,* September/October 1995, p. 56.

41. David E. Rosenbaum, Esq. First Draft: Overview of Investigation of the Group, 1983–1993.

recently expounded on the subject matter in exemplary fashion are Walter Bowart (*Operation Mind Control*, 1978), Jon Rappoport (*US Government Mind Control Experiments On Children*, 1995), and Alex Constantine (*Psychic Dictatorship in the u.s.A.*, 1995).

Conclusion

The most incriminating statement to date made by a government official as to the possible existence of Project MONARCH was extracted by Anton Chaitkin, a writer for the publication *The New Federalist*. When former CIA Director William Colby was asked directly, "What about MONARCH?" he replied angrily and ambiguously, "We stopped that between the late 1960s and the early 1970s."

Suffice to say that society, in its apparent state of cognitive dissonance, is generally in denial of the overwhelming evidence of this multifarious conspiracy. Numerous victims/survivors of Project MONARCH are in desperate need of help. However, the great majority of people are too preoccupied with themselves to show any genuine compassion toward these severely wounded individuals. Apathy has taken over the minds of the masses who choose to exist within the comforts of this world. Reality has thus become obscured by relativism and selfishness...

Extract from the book: Brice Taylor, *Thanks for the Memories* (1999).

Population Control
License to Kill … Billions

By Michael Nield

"Gradually, by selective breeding, the congenital differences between rulers and ruled will increase until they become almost different species. A revolt of the plebs would become as unthinkable as an organized insurrection of sheep against the practice of eating mutton."
—Bertrand Russell, *The Impact of Science on Society*, 1953.

"… In holding scientific research and discovery in respect, as we should, we must also be alert to the equal and opposite danger that public policy could itself become the captive of a scientific-technological elite."
—President Dwight D. Eisenhower's Farewell Address, 1961.

With the restraints of moral conventions and democracy dispensed with, the new Utopia offers the holy grail of all dictators: control over life itself. Yet, some of that control has existed for decades in spite of our notionally free and democratic societies. Science offers the great advantage that very few people can understand it. Whoever pays for its conduct and its presentation in the popular media can dictate the consensus on any given issue, simply by asserting that his committee of experts are the most distinguished. The less well funded and represented dissenters are labeled the dangerous "quacks" and "junk scientists." And this is how the petrochemical-pharmaceutical cartel has killed, injured, and sterilized millions of people over the last hundred years. The same forces that supported Hitler have continued to operate covertly ever since.

Population control is multi-faceted. It includes: reducing the number of people; eugenics; reducing intelligence levels; mind control; increasing poverty; and creating financial dependence on the pharmaceutical industry. Various facets of the population control agenda can be served simultaneously by the same device.

Facing up to this 21st century holocaust merely requires an acknowledgment of the moral position of its elevated sponsors. Some might be unashamedly evil, but most are Malthusians who believe that the there is no sanctity in human life. To "save the planet," we must kill off most of the people, so said Jacques-Yves Cousteau in the *UNESCO Courier* of November 1991:

> The damage people cause to the planet is a function of demographics—it is equal to the degree of development. One American burdens the earth much more than twenty Bangladeshes... This is a terrible thing to say. In order to stabilize world population, we must eliminate 350,000 people per day. It is a horrible thing to say, but it's just as bad not to say it.

Bertrand Russell, one of the 20th century's most eminent philosophers, said the same in his book, *The Impact of Science on Society*:

> At present the population of the world is increasing... War so far has had no great effect on this increase... I do not pretend that birth control is the only way in which population can be kept from increasing. There are others... If a Black Death could be spread throughout the world once in every generation, survivors could procreate freely without making the world too full...

Russell also supported the idea of engineering human beings to meet social requirements:

> Scientific societies are as yet in their infancy... It is to be expected that advances in physiology and psychology will give governments much more control over individual mentality than they now have even in to-

talitarian countries. Fichte laid it down from eighteen to forty in repro-
duction, in order to secure adequate cannon fodder. As a rule, artificial
insemination will be preferred to the natural method… Gradually, by
selective breeding, the congenital differences between rulers and ruled
will increase until they become almost different species. A revolt of the
plebs would become as unthinkable as an organized insurrection of
sheep against the practice of eating mutton.

The progressively dumbed down society described in *Brave New
World* is desirable to those in the ruling class who believe in "command and control." However, with the internet serving as a counter-
weight to official disinformation, we can now afford ourselves some
protection against a health catastrophe we might otherwise endure
at their hands.

Funding Population Control

Limiting population growth has been a preoccupation of the European and American elite throughout the 20th century. The Population Council was established in 1952 by John D. Rockefeller III. The
multibillion dollar World Wildlife Fund is sponsored by British and
Dutch Royalty, and the elite environmental think-tank, the Club of
Rome, counts several world leaders amongst its members. The U.N.'s
population control activities receive funding from all the major char-
itable foundations, especially the Ford Foundation and Rockefeller
Foundation. Ted Turner's $1 billion United Nations Foundation and
the $24 billion Bill and Melinda Gates Foundation are entirely de-
voted to population control activities, although they are disguised as
public health campaigns.

The United Nations Population Fund (UNFPA, formerly the United
Nations Fund for Population Activities) is the single largest international source of overt funding for population and reproductive health
programs. Since it began operations in 1969, the Fund has provided
nearly $6 billion in "assistance" to developing countries. The UNFPA
only manages one quarter of the world's population control budget
for developing countries, which is in excess of $1 billion per year.

The Netherlands, Britain, and Japan were by far the biggest funders of UNFPA in 2001, providing almost 50% of the total $396 million. Meanwhile, the U.S. Agency for International Development (USAID) gives substantially more money to population control programs than to healthcare and food assistance.

Aims and Methods

The population control agenda is presented to the public as a universal concern for planetary resources and environmental pollution and, to a lesser degree, socio-economic deprivation, women's rights, and reproductive health. Whatever the truth of these arguments, the point is that population control is coercive. The policy papers on population control contain objectives that are so extreme that coercion would certainly be needed to meet them. The 1972 benchmark environmentalist publication, *The Limits to Growth*,[42] predicted planetary meltdown by 2050 unless radical limits to population growth were imposed. In 1974, this was translated into hard U.S. national security policy by National Security Advisor Henry Kissinger. His lengthy *National Security Study Memorandum 200* (NSSM 200) laid out the aims, timescale, and methods of U.S. foreign policy for limiting the population growth of "lesser developed countries." Measures were to be taken to keep the world's population growing beyond 8 billion, meaning 500 million fewer people by year 2000 and 3 billion fewer by 2050. However, many suspect that this is nowhere near the real target of the elite and their Malthusian collaborators. The American population control think-tank, Negative Population Growth (NPG), Inc., recommended in 1992 that the population of the U.S. should be 125–150 million, requiring a 50% cut from its current level.[43] In 1995, the same think-tank published a study recommending an 80% reduction in global population.[44] In NSSM 200, Henry Kissinger stated that

42. Donella H. Meadows, Dennis L. Meadows, Jørgen Randers, William W. Behrens III. *The Limits to Growth.* Universe Books, 1972.
43. Donald Mann. "Why We Need a Smaller U.S. Population and How We Can Achieve It." NPG Position Paper, July 1992.
44. J. Kenneth Smail. "Confronting The 21st Century's Hidden Crisis: Reducing Human Numbers by 80%." NPG, May 1995.

no single approach would "solve" the population problem. Multiple and seemingly unconnected approaches would be more efficient.

Environmentalism

The environmental movement has been an important tool for justifying population reduction. Banning the pesticide DDT in the early 1970s was a huge victory for the population controllers. DDT was introduced as an insecticide in the 1940s and promised to eradicate malaria, one of the world's biggest natural killers. Despite all the scientific evidence to the contrary, the powerful environmental lobby declared it dangerous, and so it was banned. As a result, hundreds of millions of lives have been lost to malaria unnecessarily. Alexander King, president of the Club of Rome, confirmed the real purpose of the ban: "My own doubts came when DDT was introduced. In Guyana, within two years, it had almost eliminated malaria. So my chief quarrel with DDT, in hindsight, is that it has greatly added to the population problem."[45]

Public Health Policy and Western Medicine

The Drug Trust

The pharmaceutical industry is a multitrillion dollar business, and healthcare spending consumes a significant proportion of Western GDP. One family in particular has played a key role in the development of the pharmaceutical industry—The Rockefellers. The Rockefellers invested in the German chemical and pharmaceutical giant, IG Farben in the 1930s. Sterling Drug, Inc., was the main cog and largest holding company in the Rockefeller drug empire during the first half of the 20th century.[46] Today, Rockefeller-owned Bristol-Myers Squibb, Inc., accounts for nearly half of the chemotherapy sales in the world.[47]

The five leading private medical research institutes in the U.S. are

---

45. Marjorie Mazel Hecht, "Bring Back DDT, and Science With It!" *21st Century Science and Technology Magazine*, Summer 2002 issue.
46. See: Hans Ruesch, "The Drug Story," in this book.
47. Dr. Alexandra Niedzwiecki, "Terminating the Business with Disease." Presentation to the Hague Tribunal, 14 June 2003.

either controlled by or affiliated to the Rockefellers: Rockefeller University, Memorial Sloan-Kettering Cancer Center (MSKCC), Aaron Diamond AIDS Research Center (ADARC), Howard Hughes Medical Institute (HHMI), and Cold Spring Harbor Laboratories. These institutes conduct cutting edge medical research which affects the world's entire healthcare system. A brief chronology of the establishment of health and educational institutions by John D. Rockefeller:

- 1889–1909: The University of Chicago.
- 1901: The Rockefeller Institute for Medical Research, now Rockefeller University.
- 1909: Rockefeller Sanitary Commission for Eradication of Hookworm Disease.
- 1910: In partnership with the Harriman family, funded the Station for Experimental Evolution and Eugenics Records Office in Cold Spring Harbor.
- 1914: The China Medical Board.

The $65 million endowment of the Rockefeller Institute dwarfed the budget of the Public Health Service in the first three decades of 20th century.[48] Rockefeller University is a world leading center for pharmaceutical medicine. Its website boasts:

> The Rockefeller University is a world-renowned center for research and graduate education in the biomedical sciences, chemistry, bioinformatics and physics. The university's 76 laboratories conduct both clinical and basic research and study a diverse range of biological and biomedical problems... Throughout Rockefeller's history, 24 of its scientists have won Nobel Prizes, 21 have won Lasker Awards and 20 have garnered the National Medal of Science, the highest science award given by the United States..[49]

---

48. Dr. Leonard Horowitz, *Death In The Air*, Tetrahedron Publishing Group, 2001, p. 46.
49. Rockefeller University website: www.rockefeller.edu

The world's premier AIDS research institution, Aaron Diamond AIDS Research Center, is affiliated to the Rockefeller University by academic, infrastructural, and administrative ties. Established in 1991, ADARC is the world's largest private research laboratory devoted solely to biomedical research on HIV/AIDS and is currently co-leading China's largest AIDS "treatment program." Rockefeller-owned *Time* magazine voted their man at ADARC, Dr. David Ho, "Man of The Year" in 1996.

The Howard Hughes Medical Institute has worked in partnership with the Rockefeller University since 1986. Founded in 1953, at close of financial year 2002, Howard Hughes Medical Institute endowment was $10.3 billion making it the second largest philanthropy in the USA after the $24 billion Bill Gates Foundation. HHMI currently employs seven Nobel Prize winners.

The Rockefeller University has close ties with Memorial Sloan-Kettering Cancer Center. During early 1970s, Laurence S. Rockefeller sat on the board of the MSKCC and was trustee of the Sloan Foundation. The Rockefeller University archive reveals that the Rockefellers provided substantial endowment for Memorial Sloan-Kettering. The New York Cancer Hospital, founded in 1884, was one of the first hospitals devoted entirely to the research and treatment of cancer. Later known as the General Memorial Hospital for Cancer and Allied Diseases (1899–1916), and then as Memorial Hospital, it was vastly expanded and modernized in 1936 as a result of contributions by John D. Rockefeller II and the General Education Board. The Sloan foundation was founded in 1934 by Alfred P. Sloan, Chairman of General Motors. In 1945, the Sloan-Kettering Institute was created to conduct intensive research in oncology. In 1960, the MSKCC was formed to serve as an administrative umbrella for the hospital and institute. Rockefeller's modernization involved relocating Memorial to a new site just across the street from Rockefeller University. Nelson A. Rockefeller was a Member of Westchester County (NY) Board of Health from January 1933 to June 1953. Westchester became home to the Phelps Hospital founded in 1952 with Rockefeller money. With a donation of 66 acres on the Hudson River and $500,000 by the Arthur Curtis James Foundation, along with a pledge of $800,000 toward the project by John D. Rockefeller II, the new hospital was born. The Phelps Hospital is now one of the sites of the Memorial Sloan-Kettering Cancer Center.

The Station for Experimental Evolution and the Eugenics Records Office was endowed with funds from the Rockefeller and Harriman families in 1910. Since the 1970s, the renamed Cold Spring Harbor Laboratories have been home to the world's cutting edge research programs on cancer as well as research in neurobiology, plant genetics, genomics, and bioinformatics. James Watson, co-discoverer of DNA, was its director from 1969 to 1994, and it is undertaking work to map the human genome on behalf of the Human Genome Project. The early research into eugenics at Cold Spring was mirrored by the Rockefellers' funding of racial hygiene research in Germany at the Kaiser Wilhelm Institute for Psychiatry in Munich and the Kaiser Wilhelm Institute for Anthropology, Eugenics, and Human Heredity in Berlin in the late 1920s. However, the roots of this pharmaceutical stranglehold penetrate deep into the American education system. In 1910, a report was produced by the American Medical Association (AMA) that changed the course of medical history. Previously, American medical education had been unregulated and suffered a bad reputation. Seeing an opportunity, the Carnegie Foundation offered to produce guidelines and qualifications for medical schools on behalf of the AMA. The Flexner Report, named after Abraham Flexner of the Carnegie Foundation, included recommendations to strengthen courses in pharmacology. Rockefeller and Carnegie then commenced to pour money into those institutions which conformed to the new requirements. To date, Rockefeller, Carnegie, Ford, Sloan, Kellogg and other foundations have showered over a billion dollars on the medical schools of America.[50]

According to *The Drug Story* by Morris A. Bealle, an investigation into Rockefeller influence on medicine, the Rockefeller Foundation was the single largest contributor to American medical education:

---

50. G. Edward Griffin, *World Without Cancer: The Story of Vitamin* B17. American Media, 2nd edition, 1997, pp. 262-264.

Harvard, with its well-publicized medical school, has received $8,764,433 of Rockefeller's Drug Trust money, Yale got $7,927,800, Johns Hopkins $10,418,531, Washington University in St. Louis $2,842,132, New York's Columbia University $5,424,371, Cornell University $1,709,072, etc., etc.

The Rockefellers and their alumni have held key positions directing American public health, and were directly involved with the establishment of American public health institutions. In 1938, Jewish German researchers fleeing Hitler were welcomed at the newly founded National Institutes of Health (NIH) built on a private estate in Bethesda, Maryland, donated by John D. Rockefeller.[51] This is still the home of the NIH today. Nelson A. Rockefeller was Under Secretary of Department of Health, Education, and Welfare (HEW) from June 1953 to December 1954. Prior to this appointment, he was Chairman, Special Committee on Defense Organization from February to April 1953 and afterwards, Consultant to Secretary of Defense on Organization of the Department of Defense from January to April 1958. Between January 1953 and December 1958, he was Chairman of the President's Advisory Committee on Government Organization.

Rockefeller took the HEW job to reorganize the health department to meet the secrecy requirements of U.S. biological, chemical, and nuclear weapons program which required substantial testing on unwitting American and Canadian citizens as described in the section on AIDS below. Laurence S. Rockefeller was also on the board of the Community Blood Council of Greater NY, funded by the Sloan Foundation.[52] Rockefeller University faculty boasts 34 National Academy of Science members and eight of the New York Academy of Sciences' Council currently work for Rockefeller-connected companies or institutions.

---

51. Leonard Horowitz, *Death in the Air: Globalism, Terrorism & Toxic Warfare*, Medical Veritas, 2001, p. 347.
52. Leonard Horowitz, *Emerging Viruses: AIDS and Ebola: Nature, Accident, or Intentional?* Medical Veritas, 1996, p. 476.

The Business with Disease

Charges of genocide against the Drug Trust are appropriate on three counts:

1) Most pharmaceuticals do not cure diseases;
2) Pharmaceuticals kill and injure vast numbers of people;
3) Pharmaceuticals are forced upon the public by governments, and effective alternatives are denied.

Given the first two charges, it might seem impossible for the third to be accomplished in a free society. This is how it's done:

1) Laws and regulations controlling medical treatments, mainly administered by agencies such as the Food and Drug Administration in the U.S. and the Medicines Control Agency in the U.K., mandate which treatments are safe, effective, and legal;
2) Professional medical associations who license doctors dictate what treatments can be prescribed;
3) The British and European model of socialized medicine allows the government health departments to decide health policy and purchase treatment on behalf of the public which very rarely includes non-drug-based treatments;
4) Medical research bodies controlled by the Drug Trust and the government influence the policies of the previous three.

1, 2, and 3 are the enforcement arm of the cartel, whilst method 4 is the propaganda arm. In this way, Western public healthcare system is the epitome of *fascism:* the corporations use government to enforce a cartel at the expense of the public interest.

Articles in the mainstream media and medical journals have revealed the tip of the public "deathcare" iceberg. Killing 250,000 patients a year, doctors are the third leading cause of death in the U.S., according to the *Journal of American Medical Association.*[53] An edi-

---

53. Barbara Starfield, MD, MPH. "Is U.S. Health Really the Best in the World?" *Journal of American Medical Association.* 2000;284(4):483-485.

torial in *The Lancet* warned of the corruption of medicine by drug companies. The editors of this most esteemed scientific journal asked, "Just how tainted has medicine become [by pharmaceutical industry payoffs]?" They concluded, "Heavily, and damagingly so," urging doctors to "have the courage to oppose practices that bring the whole of medicine into disrepute."[54] Up to half the articles on drugs which appear in mainstream medical journals are written by ghost writers employed by drug companies, not the named authors.[55]

Congressman Dan Burton investigated vaccines for four years as Chairman of the Dan Burton Committee on Government Reform on The Status of Research into Vaccine Safety and Autism. His conclusion was that conflicts of interest at the Centers for Disease Control (CDC) were a problem, particularly on the vaccine advisory panel:

> This presents a real paradox when the CDC routinely allows scientists with blatant conflicts of interest to serve on influential advisory committees that make recommendations on new vaccines as well as policy matters... All the while these same scientists have financial ties, academic affiliations, and other vested interests in the products and companies for which they are supposed to be providing unbiased oversight.[56]

Dr. Matthias Rath, research colleague of Nobel Laureate Linus Pauling and director of Cardiovascular Research at the Linus Pauling Institute in Palo Alto, California, is a world expert in nutritional medicine.[57] On 14 June 2003, Dr. Rath filed a complaint at the International Criminal Court in The Hague against the pharmaceutical industry. The charges brought were "genocide" and other "crimes

---

54. "Just how tainted has medicine become?" *The Lancet*, Vol. 359, No. 9313; 2002.
55. Antony Barnett, "Revealed: how drug firms 'hoodwink' medical journals," *The Observer*, London, 7 December 2003.
56. Mark Benjamin, "UPI investigates: The vaccine conflict." 21 July 2003; copy on: www.tetrahedron.org/articles/vaccine_awareness/UPI_Investigates.html
57. Dr. Matthias Rath's biography on Dr. Rath Health Foundation website: www4. dr-rath-foundation.org/THE_FOUNDATION/About_Dr_Matthias_Rath/dr_rath.htm

against humanity" committed in connection with the pharmaceutical industry's business with disease:

> The accused willfully and systematically maintain cardiovascular diseases, including high blood pressure, heart failure, diabetic complications and other diseases, cancer, infectious diseases including AIDS, osteoporosis and many other of today's most common diseases that are recognized to be largely preventable by natural means. The accused have deliberately caused the unnecessary suffering and premature death of hundreds of millions of people. The accused systematically and deliberately prevent the eradication of cardiovascular disease, cancer and other diseases by obstructing and blocking the dissemination of life-saving information on the health benefits of natural non-patentable therapies. Thereby, the accused have deliberately caused further unnecessary suffering and the premature death of hundreds of millions of people. The accused deliberately and systematically expand existing diseases and creating new diseases by manufacturing and marketing pharmaceutical drugs with short-term symptomatic relief but with known and detrimental long-term side-effects. Thereby the accused have deliberately caused further unnecessary suffering and premature death of hundreds of millions of people.[58]

In 1996, the U.N. Codex Alimentarius Commission launched a worldwide initiative to restrict access to natural medicines. In August 2005, the Codex has been translated by the E.U. into the European Food Supplements Directive which became law removing thousands of vitamin formulations from the shops and dramatically cutting the dosage of many others. It was followed by the Herbal Medicines Directive which prevents any new herbal formulas ever coming onto the market and removes any herbal product which doesn't have a proven track record in the E.U. The Pharmaceuticals Directive seeks to expand

---

58. Dr. Matthias Rath, "Complaint Against Genocide and Other Crimes Against Humanity Committed in Connection with the Pharmaceutical 'Business with Disease' and the Recent War against Iraq." See: www4.dr-rath-foundation.org/ The_Hague/complaint/

the scope of the drug classification. In its current wording, even food or water can be included as a substance which "restores, corrects, or modifies physiological functions."

The banning of over-the-counter natural medicine creates a two-tier planetary health system as the E.U. laws are imposed in other countries under World Trade Organization's "harmonization" rules which will include America. Natural medicines will be available on prescription only for those that can afford to pay for private consultations whilst the state-run healthcare systems will continue to prescribe pharmaceuticals to the public.

The controlling stake in the pharmaceutical industry is held by the same tiny cabal that controls all other major industries. They are committed to planetary depopulation, as their policy papers show. It is not, therefore, just about making money.

Cancer

One in three Europeans and one in two Americans will get cancer. Ten million people a year die of cancer worldwide.[59] Despite the trillions of dollars spent on orthodox research and treatment for cancer, the medical establishment is no further forward in finding a cure. The reason is, of course, that the cancer industry is a hugely profitable population control program which depends upon patented drugs.

The book *World Without Cancer: The Story of Vitamin B17* by G. Edward Griffin was first published in 1974. The foreword to the 1997 edition states that absolutely nothing has changed since the first edition, except the actors in the plot. The book details the astonishing fraud and cover-up of the effectiveness of vitamin B17 (laetrile), not least by the Rockefellers' Memorial Sloan-Kettering Cancer Center. For five years between 1972 and 1977, the effectiveness of laetrile was tested by Dr. Kanematsu Sugiara at the MSKCC. On 13 June 1973, he produced a report which strongly indicated its anticancer properties. This did not please his employer who then set about denigrating his findings saying that no one else could reproduce them. By 1977, the propaganda war was won. However, in November 1997, Ralph

---

59. Dr. Alexandra Niedzwiecki. Presentation to the Hague Tribunal, *op. cit.*

Moss, the Assistant Director of Public Affairs, who wrote the propaganda, did an extraordinary thing: he held his own press conference at which he named the MSKCC officials who had collaborated in the massive laetrile cover-up. He was fired the next day, and the media soon forgot all about it.[60]

Since the FDA banned laetrile in 1971, thousands of Americans have traveled to Mexico and Germany every year to be treated with it. American doctors can have their licenses taken away for prescribing laetrile, or even face imprisonment in California due to its "anti-quack" cancer legislation. In the U.K., it is illegal for anyone other than registered medical practitioners to claim they can cure or treat cancer.[61] Unfortunately, it is the Rockefeller/IG Farben monopoly treatment of cancer which is quackery: there is no evidence that chemotherapy or radiotherapy increase life expectancy. In fact, both are extremely toxic and often lethal treatments which themselves destroy the patient's immune system and cause cancer and death.

Dr. Lorraine Day is an internationally acclaimed orthopedic trauma surgeon and bestselling author. She spent 15 years on the faculty of the University of California School of Medicine in San Francisco as Associate Professor and Vice Chairman of the Department of Orthopedics. She was also Chief of Orthopedic Surgery at San Francisco General Hospital and is recognized worldwide as an AIDS expert. Ten years ago, she contracted breast cancer and reached the terminal stage. However, she refused orthodox treatment and devised for herself a ten-point plan which didn't involve drugs or even vitamin supplements. Knowing that cancer is the consequence of a dysfunctional immune system, poor diet, and lifestyle and environmental factors, she cured herself by addressing these issues. Dr. Day, like many thousands of others, is alive and well today by taking matters into her own hands. She is roundly attacked in the mainstream press for her cru-

60. G. Edward Griffin. *World Without Cancer: The Story of Vitamin B17*. American Media, 2nd ed., 1997, pp. 40-41, 59-50.
61. The Cancer Act 1939, U.K. See: www.whale.to/cancer/act.html; news.bbc.co.uk/2/hi/uk news/wales/3044315.stm

sade against the fraud of the cancer industry and the drug industry in general. Her website is at *www.drday.com.*

Vaccination: The Weapon of Choice

It seems illogical that self-proclaimed population control advocates would spend billions of dollars on vaccination programs trying to save the lives of millions of people in the Third World. The grim reality is that they are covertly murdering and sterilizing these poor people under the guise of public health. Launched in 1999, the Global Alliance for Vaccines and Immunization (GAVI) is a partnership of the who's who in population control: the Rockefeller Foundation, the $24 billion Bill and Melinda Gates Foundation, the United Nations Foundation (a $1 billion endowment by Ted Turner), the World Bank, the World Health Organization and Western governments.

The stated mission of GAVI and the Vaccine Fund is to ensure that "all the world's children have equal access to lifesaving vaccines." Unfortunately, the more malnourished a child is the more likely it is to suffer a severe reaction to immune-suppressing vaccinations, especially when they are given in combination. Even the American Vaccination Adverse Event Reporting Systems (VAERS), set up in 1990, gives some indication of the carnage caused by vaccines. 90% of all adverse reactions go unreported to VAERS, and chronic conditions which emerge months or years later, such as autism, autoimmune diseases, allergies, cancer, and neurodevelopment disorders, are not officially recognized as consequences of vaccinations anyway. The report by United Press International should be read bearing this in mind:

> As of the end of last year, the system contained 244,424 total reports of possible reactions to vaccines, including 99,145 emergency room visits, 5,149 life-threatening reactions, 27,925 hospitalizations, 5,775 disabilities, and 5,309 deaths, according to data compiled by Dr. Mark Geier, a vaccine researcher in Silver Spring, MD. The data represents roughly 1 billion doses of vaccines, according to Geier.[62]

---

62. Mark Benjamin, *op. cit.*

An investigative report by Roman Bystrianyk for *HealthSentinel.com* shows that there is little epidemiological evidence for the contribution of vaccines to the wide-scale reduction in death rates from infectious diseases.[63] The *Vital Statistics of the United States,* published by the Bureau of the Census and the u.s. Department of Health, contain death rates from infectious diseases. From 1900 to 1963, when the measles vaccine was introduced, death rates from measles had declined from 13.3 per 100,000 to 0.2 per 100,000—a 98% decrease. From 1900 to 1949, death rates from whooping cough declined from 12.2 per 100,000 to 0.5 per 100,000—a 96% decrease. From 1900 to 1949, death rates from diphtheria declined from 40.3 per 100,000 to 0.4 per 100,000—a 99% decrease.

Mortality data in England and Wales provided by the Office of National Statistics in 1997 shows an identical picture. From 1850 to 1968, when the measles vaccine was introduced, death rates from measles had declined from a range of 52.11 to 26.6 per 100,000 to 0.11 per 100,000—a range of 99.6% to 99.8% decrease. From 1860 to 1955, death rates from whooping cough declined from a range of 43.73 to 60.86 per 100,000 to 0.2 per 100,000—a 99.5% to 99.7% decrease.

Also note that scarlet fever and typhoid were eliminated in both countries without *any* vaccination program.

Public health experts have long recognized these facts. Thomas McKeown (1912–1988) was professor of social medicine in the University of Birmingham Medical School between 1950 and 1978. He is still regarded as a major social philosopher of medicine and known for his important works on epidemiology and the practice and purpose of medicine. His conclusion was that infectious diseases were declining well before widespread vaccination and that "reductions in deaths associated with infectious diseases (air-, water-, and food-borne diseases) cannot have been brought about by medical advances, since such diseases were declining long before effective means were available to combat them."

---

63. Roman Bystrianyk, "The Real Truth: Vaccination Inefficacy in the Reduction/ Elimination of Infectious Diseases." 23 February 2003. www.tetrahedron.org/ articles/vaccine_awareness/vaccination_inefficacy.html

A paper published in *The Lancet* in January 1977 by the Department of Community Medicine also indicated that vaccinations were not responsible for the decline in mortality:

> Vaccination, beginning on small scale in some places around 1948 and on a national scale in 1957, did not affect the rate of decline if it be assumed that one attack usually confers immunity, as in most major communicable diseases of childhood. ... The steady decline of whooping cough between 1930 and 1957 is predictive of a linear exponential decay characteristic of a general and progressive lessening in the volume and spread of infection among the susceptible population. With this pattern well established before 1957, there is no evidence that vaccination played a major role in the decline in incidence and mortality in the trend of events.

An even more recent editorial statement from the *Journal of Pediatrics,* in December 1999, declared that proper sanitation was largely responsible for the early large declines in infectious diseases:

> ... The largest historical decrease in morbidity and mortality caused by infectious disease was experienced not with the modern antibiotic and vaccine era, but after the introduction of clean water and effective sewer systems.

Again, in the August 2001 edition of the *American Journal of Infection Control*, epidemiologists concluded that,

> ... except for the smallpox vaccination, which was introduced in 1798 and made compulsory in England in 1853, the overall contribution of medical innovations to the health revolution of the 1800s is difficult to validate.
>
> Diphtheria, tetanus, and pertussis vaccine arrived on the scene only after disease mortality rates already had been reduced significantly; measles, rubella, and polio vaccines did not become available until the middle of the 20th century.

Immune Suppression

Because they do not trigger a proper immune response, vaccinations give live viruses and other live vaccine contaminants a head start in the body. Normally, microorganisms have to pass through the mucous membranes in the mouth and gastrointestinal tract, which are lined with Immunoglobulin A. Interaction with IgA triggers a cellular immune response which precedes the antibody/humoral response. Injected microorganisms bypass the mucousal/cellular immune system and directly trigger the antibody-producing plasma cells in the bone marrow. This is why vaccine manufactures add immune system stimulating "adjuvants" such as aluminium, lipopolysaccharide, and squalene. Live microorganisms also take advantage of significant immune suppression caused by the vaccination itself. Research found that 20% of measles vaccines recipients have chronic measles infections in their brains later in life indicating that live virus vaccines create greater risk of developing the disease.[64] In the *New England Journal of Medicine* of July 1994, a study found that over 80% of children under 5 years of age who had contracted whooping cough had been fully vaccinated against it.[65]

Dr. Archie Kalokerinos is a Life Fellow of the Royal Society for Health, a Fellow of the International Academy of Preventive Medicine, Fellow of the Australasian College of Biomedical Scientists, Fellow of the Hong Kong Medical Technology Association, and a Member of the New York Academy of Sciences. In 1978, he was awarded the A.M.M. (Australian Medal of Merit) for "outstanding scientific research." On the subject of vaccines he comments:

> My final conclusion after forty years or more in this business [medicine] is that the unofficial policy of the World Health Organization and … [other vaccine-promoting] organizations is one of murder and genocide… You cannot immunize sick children, malnourished children, and

---

64. Dr. Russell Blaylock, author of *Health and Nutrition Secrets That Can Save Your Life* (2006), interviewed by Dr. Stanley Monteith on *Radio Liberty*, 2 December 2003. www.radioliberty.com
65. Dr. Joseph Mercola. "Vaccination Statistics." www.mercola.com/article/vaccines/statistics.htm

expect to get away with it. You'll kill far more children than would have died from natural infection. It was similar with the measles vaccination. They went through Africa, South America and elsewhere, and vaccinated sick and starving children… They thought they were wiping out measles, but most of those susceptible to measles died from some other disease that they developed as a result of being vaccinated. The vaccination reduced their immune levels and acted like an infection. Many got septicemia, gastroenteritis, etc., or made their nutritional status worse, and they died from malnutrition. So there were very few susceptible infants left alive to get measles. It's one way to get good statistics, kill all those that are susceptible, which is what they literally did.[66]

American children receive up to forty vaccinations before the age of two. Dr. H. H. Fudenberg, world-renowned immunologist with hundreds of publications to his credit, made the following comments:

One vaccine decreases cell-mediated immunity by 50%, two vaccines by 70%… All triple vaccines (MMR, DTAP) markedly impair cell-mediated immunity, which predisposes to recurrent viral infections.[67]

Like HIV, the measles virus is particularly immune suppressing, hence the danger of the live virus measles vaccine. In 2001, GAVI launched an initiative to vaccinate 200 million children in sub-Saharan Africa against measles, despite the fact that HIV infection was rampant there.

Vaccine Contaminants

As well as the dangerous assault on fragile immune systems by the vaccine's active ingredients, there are live contaminants in vaccines. Microorganism contamination is a relatively common finding in many commercial vaccines. One study in the journal *Vaccine,* in 1986, found that about 6% of commercial vaccines tested were contaminated with a tiny bacteria called mycoplasma. Most U.S. military personnel de-

---

66. Dr. Kalokerinos, MD, quotes: www.whale.to/m/kalokerinos9.html
67. Harold E. Buttram, MD; Susan Kreider, RN; Alan R. Yurko. "Vaccines and Genetic Mutation." 11 October 2002; www.freeyurko.bizland.com/vacgen.html

ployed to the Gulf in 1990 received up to 30 vaccinations in a two to three-day period, some probably experimental and administered without proper informed consent. Recent studies by the Institute of Molecular Medicine found that nearly 40% of veterans with Gulf War Illness were infected with mycoplasma *fermentans*.[68] 100% of Gulf War Illness patients who developed the motor neuron disease, amyotrophic lateral sclerosis, tested positive for systemic mycoplasma infection.[69]

The polio vaccine administered to 30 million Americans during the late fifties and early sixties was contaminated with the monkey virus sv40. This is believed to be responsible for an epidemic of cancers.[70] When sv40 was discovered in rhesus monkey kidney cells during the early 1960s, the manufacturers switched rapidly to cells from African green monkeys. However, Dr. John Martin, an FDA scientist, discovered in 1972 that these cells were also contaminated, this time with a cytomegalovirus. His requests to have the vaccine properly tested have gone unanswered by the FDA, because the manufacturers can hide behind "proprietary interests."

Vaccines for Sterilization

The World Health Organization has a twenty-year history of developing contraceptive vaccines. These work by creating immunity to the body's own fertility hormone, human chorionic gonadotrophin (hCG).[71] A BBC documentary entitled *Horizon: The Human Laboratory,*

68. Dr. Garth L. Nicolson and Dr. Nancy L. Nicolson. "The Vaccine Controversy: Why Full Informed Consent Must Be Instituted for All Vaccines." February 2001. www.immed.org/autoimmune/06.16.12%20pdfs%20updates/Crim-Pol-Vaccines-01.2.2.pdf

69. Garth L. Nicolson, PHD; Marwan Y. Nasralla, PHD; Joerg Haier, MD, PHD; John Pomfret, PHD. "High Frequency of Systemic Mycoplasmal Infections in Gulf War Veterans and Civilians with Amyotrophic Lateral Sclerosis (ALS)." *Journal of Clinical Neuroscience* 2002; 9:525-529.

70. Dr. Joseph Mercola. "Simian Virus 40 DNA Found in U.S. Children." articles.mercola.com/sites/articles/archive/2008/01/02/simian-virus-40-dna-found-in-us-children.aspx

71. Gordon L. Ada (Editor), P. D. Griffin (Editor), *Vaccines for Fertility Regulation: The Assessment of Their Safety and Efficacy.* Cambridge University Press, 1991.

aired 5 November 1995, revealed that the WHO started using these vaccines to sterilize women in the mid-1990s. They got caught giving it to women without informed consent in the Philippines, by putting in the tetanus shots. After the recipients of the vaccine started having miscarriages, a study conducted by the Philippine Medical Association on behalf of the Philippine Department of Health revealed that almost 20% of the tetanus vaccine sampled positive for hCG.

A UNICEF campaign to vaccinate Nigeria's youth against polio may have been a front for sterilizing the nation, according to Dr. Haruna Kaita, a pharmaceutical scientist. In March 2004, he reported that, using WHO-recommended technologies like gas chromatography (GC) and radioimmunoassay, he found evidence of serious contamination.

"Some of the things we discovered in the vaccines are harmful, toxic; some have direct effects on the human reproductive system," he said. Asked why he thought manufacturers would do this, he replied: "These manufacturers, or promoters of these harmful things, have a secret agenda which only further research can reveal. Secondly, they have always taken us in the Third World for granted, thinking we don't have the capacity, knowledge, and equipment to conduct tests that would reveal such contaminants. And, very unfortunately, they also have people to defend their atrocities within our midst, and worse still, some of these are supposed to be our own professionals who we rely on to protect our interests.[72]

Mercury

First manufactured in the 1930s, thimerosal is a mercury compound containing 49.6% of ethylmercury by weight. Since then, it has been used in some multi-dose vaccines as a preservative. Autism was relatively uncommon before 1990, averaging around 1 in 10,000 American children. Today it averages 1 in 150.[73] 7 out of 10 autistic children have an IQ below 70 points, low enough to create "learning difficul-

---

72. "UNICEF Nigerian Polio Vaccine Contaminated with Sterilizing Agents Scientist Finds." *Life Site*, 11 March 2004. www.lifesitenews.com/news/unicef-nigerian-polio-vaccine-contaminated-with-sterilizing-agents-scientis
73. www.safeminds.org/mercury/

ties." Researchers believe that when the number of vaccines given to children was increased in 1990, the public health agencies failed to take into account the cumulative mercury exposure.

A United Press International investigation into the vaccine controversy reported that, depending on what vaccines a child got during that period, a visit to the doctor during the 1990s may have exposed some children to 125 times the limit on mercury set by the Environmental Protection Agency (EPA). Since the mid-1980s, the CDC has doubled the number of vaccines children get, up to nearly 40 doses before age 2.[74] On 7 July 1999, the American Academy of Pediatrics and the U.S. Public Health Service issued a joint statement calling for the removal of thimerosal from vaccines following a risk assessment by the FDA. Although manufacturers did take steps to remove it from many vaccines, there is no requirement for them to do so, because the CDC will not take action. Dr. Mark Geier, an expert witness on vaccine cases, states that major manufacturers are still using thimerosal and that children were being injected with more mercury than ever in 2003.[75] Fluzone by Aventis Pasteur is provided in multi-dose vials that still contain 25 mcg of thimerosal—25 times the safe level of mercury suggested by the FDA.[76]

The Institute of Medicine which advises the CDC on this issue refuses to acknowledge the dangers of thimerosal. This is in spite of Dr. Mark Gaier's study published in the *Journal of American Physicians and Surgeons* in April 2003,[77] which concluded that there is a strong link between thimerosal exposure and neurodevelopment disorders such as autism, speech impediments, and attention deficit disorder. Gaier noted that one in eight American children requires special ed-

74. Mark Benjamin, *op cit.*
75. Kelly Patricia O'Meara. "CDC Study Raises Level of Suspicion," *Insight on the News.* 8 December 2003. www.insightmag.com
76. "Mothering Magazine warns parents about mercury in flu vaccines." Press Release, 5 July 2004. www.safeminds.org/pressroom/press_releases/MotherMagazinePressRelease.pdf
77. Mark R. Geier, MD, PHD., David A. Geier. "Thimerosal in Childhood Vaccines, Neurodevelopment Disorders, and Heart Disease in the United States." *Journal of American Physicians and Surgeons*, Vol. 8, No. 1, Spring 2003. www.jpands.org/vol8no1/geier.pdf

ucation due to brain impairment and that number is expected to rise to one in five.

In February 2000, Dr. Thomas Verstraeten of the National Immunization Program of the CDC produced an analysis of the CDC's Vaccine Safety Datalink, a patient record database that includes information on vaccinated children who developed neurological disorders. These findings were never made public, but they were discussed at a secret CDC conference held on 7–8 June 2000 at the Simpsonwood Retreat Center, Norcross, GA. This was top level assembly of 51 scientists and physicians of which five represented vaccine manufacturers GlaxoSmithKline, Merck, Wyeth, North American Vaccine, and Aventis Pasteur. Minutes of the conference were obtained by Congressman David Weldon through a freedom of information request.[78] Verstraeten's findings showed a risk of autism 2.48 times greater for infants who received the highest amounts of mercury in vaccines. The delegates agreed to keep these findings secret and went on to discuss how to manipulate the data to conceal the association. In November 2003, Verstraeten et al published a study in *Pediatrics* which denied the association. The journal did not disclose that, since the meeting in 2000, Verstraeten worked for GlaxoSmithKline. In December 2003, Congressman Weldon got Dr. Mark Geier access to the Datalink database and he was able to conclude that the earlier findings were correct.[79]

Vaccine Adjuvants

Dr. Russell Blaylock is a neurosurgeon and expert on excitotoxins. He warns that mercury is not the only vaccine additive which can cause brain damage, including autism.[80]

---

78. Congressman Dave Weldon, MD. Letter to the CDC, 31 October 2003.
79. Lisa Reagan. "Institute of Medicine Meets a Second Time to Review Vaccine/Autism Link". *Mothering Magazine*.
80. Russell L. Blaylock, MD. "Vaccination Dangers Can Kill You or Ruin Your Life." 12 May 2004. articles.mercola.com/sites/articles/archive/2004/05/12/vaccination-dangers.aspx. Also: Blaylock. "Chronic Microglial Activation and Excitotoxicity Secondary to Excessive Immune Stimulation: Possible Factors in Gulf War Syndrome and Autism". *Journal of American Physicians and Surgeons*, Vol. 9, No. 2, Summer 2004. www.whale.to/a/pdf/blaylock.pdf

Substances called adjuvants are added to vaccines in order to stimulate an immune response. These include squalene, aluminium, and lipopolysaccharide. The problem with current heavy vaccination schedules is that these substances remain in the tissues, continually stimulating the immune system. This is particularly bad for the brain, because its immune system cells, called microglia, once activated, begin to move about the nervous system, secreting numerous immune chemicals (called cytokines and chemokines) and pouring out an enormous amount of free radicals in an effort to kill invading organisms. The problem is, there are no invading organisms. The microglia have been tricked by the vaccine into believing there are. Unlike the body's immune system, the microglia also secrete two other chemicals that are very destructive of brain cells and their connecting processes. These chemicals, glutamate and quinolinic acid, are called excitotoxins. They also dramatically increase free radical generation in the brain. Studies of patients have shown that levels of these two excitotoxins can rise to very dangerous levels in the brain following viral and bacterial infections of the brain. High quinolinic acid levels in the brain are thought to be the cause of the dementia seen with HIV infection.

A recent study by the world-renowned immunologist Dr. H. Hugh Fudenberg, found that adults vaccinated yearly for five years in a row with the flu vaccine had a 10-fold increased risk of developing Alzheimer's disease. He attributes this to the mercury and aluminium in the vaccine. Interestingly, both of these metals have been shown to activate microglia and increase excitotoxicity in the brain.

Vaccines and Sudden Infant Death and Shaken Baby Syndromes

In the early 1970s, the medical establishment came up with a diagnosis of Sudden Infant Death Syndrome (SIDS) and Shaken Baby Syndrome (SBS) to hide the fact that vaccines might be killing thousands of babies all over the world every year. After their baby fell victim in 1997, Alan and Francine Yurko launched "The Yurko Project"[81] to expose the real cause of their son's death. They successfully rallied an army of scientists and doctors from around the world and, in August 2004, after

---

81. www.freeyurko.bizland.com

Alan had spent seven years in prison, they overturned his wrongful conviction for shaking his son to death. A series of high profile cases in the U.K. have thrown the whole diagnoses of shaken baby syndrome and other spurious allegations of infanticide into disrepute.[82]

Most of the parents who contact the Yurko Project for help state that their child's problems began within days of vaccination. This reflects the official data on SIDS and SBS. There are approximately 2500 SIDS cases and 1300 SBS cases per year in the U.S. The Center for Disease control acknowledges that the peak age for SIDS—2 to 4 months—coincides with the first round of vaccinations.[83] The bacterial vaccines, which contain endotoxin, DTap and Hib, are particularly suspect... The mean average age for SBS cases is 2.2 months.[84]

Autoimmune and Inflammatory Diseases

The connection between vaccination and inflammatory disease is strong. Inflammatory diseases plaguing Western nations include: type one diabetes, rheumatoid arthritis, asthma, hay fever and other allergies, multiple sclerosis, Guillain-Barre, amyotrophic lateral sclerosis/motor neuron disease, Stevens-Johnson's syndrome, lupus, Alzheimer's, Parkinson's, Huntington's, Crohn's colitis, and irritable bowel syndrome.

In the U.S., asthma in children has doubled in the last twenty years coinciding with the doubling of childhood vaccines.[85] In New Zealand, there was a 60% increase in juvenile diabetes following a massive hepatitis B vaccination program for newborns. In Finland, the incidence of juvenile diabetes increased 147% in children under five after the introduction of three new vaccines for children in the

---

82. Viera Scheibner, PHD. "Shaken Baby Syndrome Diagnosis On Shaky Ground." *Journal of Australasian College of Nutritional & Environmental Medicine*, Vol. 20 No. 2; August 2001. See also: "Wider cot deaths review considered," BBC News, 20 January 2004. news.bbc.co.uk/2/hi/uk_news/3412307.stm

83. "Sudden Infant Death Syndrome (SIDS) and Vaccines," CDC website: www.cdc.gov/vaccinesafety/Concerns/sids_faq.html

84. Karen M. Barlow, MRCP (U.K.), Royal Hospital for Sick Children. "Study Reveals Shaken Baby Syndrome Statistics in Scotland." National Center on Shaken Baby Syndrome. www.dontshake.org/sbs.php?topNavID=3&subNavID=27&navID=93

85. Mark Benjamin, *op cit.*

late 1970s. Then, in the late 1980s, addition of a live MMR vaccine and an experimental vaccine (HIB) resulted in another 62% increase in the incidence of juvenile diabetes in children 3 months or older who received the new multiple vaccines. Interestingly, a former NIH investigator, Dr. J. B. Classen, has proposed that the increase in type 1 juvenile diabetes associated with multiple childhood vaccines may be avoidable by changing the regimen by which multiple vaccines are given in childhood.[86] Merck & Co's documentation on the adverse reactions to its hepatitis B vaccine is published in the Physician's Desk Reference. Some of the inflammatory and autoimmune diseases listed include Guillain-Barre, multiple sclerosis, arthritis, lupus and Stevens-Johnson's syndrome.[87]

In 1998, France became the first country to terminate a hepB vaccine program. The French Ministry of Health acted, when complaints of multiple sclerosis, rheumatoid arthritis and other illnesses in patients who received the hepB vaccine were reported. Up to 900 cases of multiple sclerosis may have been linked to the vaccine.[88]

In 2002, the "Madsen study" of 537,304 children in Denmark concluded that there was no link between the MMR vaccine and autism. This study is cited by public health agencies around the world as definitive proof that MMR is safe. However, in Autumn 2004, an article was published, which contradicted these findings. The Madsen study monitored the progress of vaccinated children in Denmark for only four years. Dr. Fouad Yazbak and Dr. G. S. Goldman looked at the same data, but over a longer period of time, and found that prevalence of autism among children aged from 5 to 9 stood at 8.38 cases per 100,000 in the pre-vaccine years 1980 to 1986, and then rose to 71.43 cases by the year 2000.[89]

86. Dr. Garth L. Nicolson and Dr. Nancy L. Nicolson. "The Vaccine Controversy: Why Full Informed Consent Must be Instituted for All Vaccines." Criminal Politics 2003. www.immed.org/autoimmune/06.16.12%20pdfs%20updates/CrimPol-Vaccines-01.2.2.pdf
87. Horowitz, Death in the Air, p. 276.
88. "Report Criticizes French Hepatitis Vaccination Campaign," Reuters, 20 November 2002. See: www.vaccinetruth.org/france1.htm
89. G. S. Goldman, PHD., F. E. Yazbak, MD, FAAP. "An Investigation of the Association

SmithKline Beecham produced a vaccine for Lyme disease called Lymerix in 1996. By October 2000, it had been given to 1.4 million people, according to the Centers for Disease Control. However, the company pulled the vaccine off the market in February 2002 after large numbers of recipients developed chronic arthritic symptoms.[90]

The science of immunology is extremely complex, but vaccination critics believe that the fundamental problem with vaccines is the injection of foreign substances directly into the body. Heavy childhood vaccination schedules may permanently skew the immune system towards a humoral response. Immune systems biased towards humoral immunity are associated with autoimmune diseases and allergies.

Autoimmune diseases can also be caused by the virus itself as well as by modification to the cellular/humoral balance of the immune system. Viruses and other live vaccine contaminants such as mycoplasmas frequently have surface proteins which are similar to those in the human body, particularly in the brain and nervous system.[91] It is well established in the scientific literature that genes can be transferred between microorganisms and human cells. Any slight genetic changes to the surface proteins of human cells by genetic transfer from microorganisms or vice-versa can lead to an autoimmune response.[92]

Inflammatory Disease and Cancer

Many adverse reactions to vaccines can prove fatal in the long term. Dr. Russell Blaylock points out the relationship between inflammatory disease and cancer. Medical research found that 76% of cancer

Between MMR Vaccination and Autism in Denmark." *Journal of American Physicians and Surgeons,* 2004; 9(3):70-75. www.jpands.org/vol9no3/goldman.pdf

90. Horowitz, *Death in the Air,* p. 277.

91. G. L. Nicolson et al. "The Pathogenesis And Treatment Of Mycoplasmal Infections." *Antimicrob. Infect. Dis. Newsl.* 1999; 17(11): 81-88. See: www.immed.org/illness/infectious_disease_research.html

92. Dr. Leonard Horowitz, "Autism, Allergy, Asthma and Vaccine Induced Autoimmunity." www.tetrahedron.org/articles/vaccine_awareness/vaccine_induced_autoimmunity.html. Also: Harold E. Buttram, MD; Susan Kreider, R.N.; Alan R. Yurko. "Vaccines and Genetic Mutation." 11 October 2002. www.freeyurko.bizland.com/vacgen.html

patients had developed an inflammatory disease 7–13 years before.[93] These findings were the cover story of *Time Magazine* on 23 February 2004. Inflammation produces large amounts of free radicals that damage DNA.[94]

The Future of Vaccination

In July 2004, *The Independent* newspaper reported that vaccines which block sensations of euphoria associated with narcotics and smoking are under development. The British government has backed the research in the hope that soon doctors will be able to vaccinate children to prevent them experiencing the pleasure associated with taking drugs. Given that vaccines are already strongly suspected of reducing children's intelligence, any attempt to interfere with their emotional responses has to be viewed with concern. Will the new vaccines create a generation of emotionally impotent automatons? Orwell predicted that the Party would abolish the orgasm, after all.[95]

Mind Control Technology

America's consumption of psychotropic drugs is so great that Prozac has made its way into the water supply and is contaminating fresh water fish. Ritalin is prescribed to about two million American children. It has become the standard way for teachers and parents to deal with unruly children even to the point where children are being threatened with expulsion or being taken into care if they do not take it.[96] Ritalin is an ideal mind control drug, because it suppresses the natural energy and spirit of young people, often leaving them robotic, lethargic, depressed, or withdrawn. It also introduces the idea

93. Dr. Russell Blaylock, interviewed by Dr. Stanley Monteith on *Radio Liberty*, 2 December 2003.
94. Christine Gorman, Alice Park, Kristina Dell. "Health: The Fires Within." *Time*, 23 Feb. 2004. content.time.com/time/magazine/article/0,9171,993419,00.html
95. Sophie Goodchild, Steve Bloomfield. "Children to get jabs against drug addiction." *The Independent*, 25 July 2004. www.independent.co.uk/news/uk/crime/children-to-get-jabs-against-drug-addiction-554368.html
96. "Schools in row over Ritalin." *BBC News*, 24 July 2003. news.bbc.co.uk/2/hi/health/3093087.stm

at an early age that drugs are an acceptable way of dealing with social problems.

Europe is not being left behind on the quest for "soma." Nearly one in four French people are on tranquillizers, antidepressants, antipsychotics, or other mood-altering prescription drugs. An average of 40% of men and women aged over 70 in France, as well as some 4% of all children under nine, were routinely prescribed at least one of this class of dependence-creating drugs.[97]

Prozac and other SSRI (selective serotonin reuptake inhibitors) are capable of inducing psychosis and suicidal depression. In the U.K., certain SSRI have recently been banned from being prescribed to children after a string of suicides. The active ingredient in Prozac and many other drugs is *fluoride*, which has been linked to brain damage and loss of IQ.

Brain Microchips

The future of mind control, and even body control, lies in electronic implants which are currently under development. Some recent news articles describe medical applications of microchips with mind and body control potential. The BBC reported that patients with chronic migraines could one day have an electric device implanted into their foreheads to control the pain. Doctors in the United States have already used the treatment successfully on one woman who was suffering from constant headaches.[98] The BBC also reported that U.S. scientists writing in *Nature Materials* describe a drug-containing microchip which can be implanted in the body. This releases the medication slowly, so the patient no longer has to take any pills.[99]

With satellite-linked implantable microchips being developed by Applied Digital Solutions, Inc., the prospect of remote controlled medical implants may not be too distant.

97. Jon Henley. "Depressed, moi? Why the French are driven to drugs". *The Guardian*, 8 Nov. 2003. www.theguardian.com/world/2003/nov/08/france.jonhenley1
98. "Implant could cure migraines." BBC *News*, 24 February 2003. news.bbc.co.uk/2/hi/health/2772885.stm
99. Ania Lichtarowicz, "Microchip could do away with pills." BBC *News*, 19 October 2003. news.bbc.co.uk/2/hi/health/3205800.stm

Electromagnetic Mind Control

Congressman Dennis Kucinich's 2001 Preservation of Space Act called for a ban on "the use of land-based, sea-based, or space-based systems using radiation, electromagnetic, psychotronic, sonic, laser, or other energies directed at individual persons or targeted populations for the purpose of information war, mood management or mind control of such persons or populations." Kucinich was referring to technologies he had learned about during his chairmanship of the House Armed Services Oversight Committee.

Private researchers, such as Dr. Nick Begich, have turned up some remarkably frank discussions of mind control published by the U.S. military. "The Mind Has No Firewall" by Timothy L. Thomas, published in the spring 1998 issue of the U.S. Army War College's quarterly *Parameters,* described decades of research in the U.S. and the Soviet Union focused on manipulating human behavior. Propaganda is considered a key tool of psychotronic warfare, including tactics such as "information overload." Certain electronic devices are completely undetectable. This can put viewers of television or computer screens into a trance and change their perceptions.

Dr. Begich obtained documents from the Scientific Advisory Board of the Air Force, in which researchers envisage the development of electromagnetic weapons which can prevent voluntary muscular movements, control emotions, produce sleep, interfere with memory, and delete experience. Writing in the military journal *Orienteer* of February 1997, Russian army Major I. Chernishev describes the development of a psychotronic generator capable of broadcasting through telephone lines, TV, radio networks, supply pipes, and incandescent lights.[100] Even more disturbing is the use of high-power microwaves in the gigahertz range to beam sounds directly into human brains and literally talk to people. As early as 1933, Soviet scientists had discovered that microwave irradiation caused central nervous system changes and affected behavior even at low intensity. Physiological dis-

100. Horowitz, *Death in the Air,* pp. 301-304. Also see Dr. Begich's article "Star Wars, Star Trek and Killing Politely" at www.earthpulse.com/src/subcategory. asp?catid=1&subcatid=5

turbances include immune suppression, hormonal imbalances, sleep impairment and sterility.[101]

The new British police radio system called TETRA uses pulsed microwaves at 17.6 Hz, a frequency in the 13 Hz to 20 Hz beta range of the human brain's electrical activity. Unlike ordinary mobile phone masts, which only respond on demand and produce a continuous microwave signal, TETRA masts are permanently active. TETRA is a £3-billion system initiated by the Home Office and adopted by all British police forces since the end of 2005.[102]

Interference with the alpha wave of brain activity is threatened by the U.S. Defense Department's High Frequency Active Auroral Research Program (HAARP), a gigantic electromagnetic frequency generator in Alaska:

> The alpha-wave frequency of the human brain is known to be between eight and twelve hertz… The ionospheric wave-guide oscillates at eight hertz, making it a good harmonic carrier of low frequency sound (LFS) waves. In the June 17, 1976, issue of *New Scientist*, Dr. Frank Barnaby, Director of the Stockholm International Peace Research Institute, warned that if methods could be devised to produce greater field strengths of such low-frequency oscillations, either by natural or artificial means, then it might become possible to impair performance of a large group of people in selected regions over extended periods.[103]

Equivalent projects are the European Incoherent Scatter Radar site (EISCAT) in Tromsoe, Norway, and SURA in Nizhny Novgorod, Russia.

Junk Food

The Western diet is a "slow kill" which largely goes undetected. Three major components—sugar, caffeine, and hydrogenated vegetable oils—open the door for every type of disease by playing havoc with

101. Horowitz, *Death in the Air*, p. 335.
102. "Does TETRA pulse? Does it matter?" TETRAWatch website: www.tetrawatch.net/tetra/pulse.php
103. Horowitz, *Death in the Air*, p. 223.

the body's metabolism and immune system. On top of this are the neurotoxic and cancer-causing flavor enhancers which are added to the majority of processed foods and soft drinks, especially in the U.S. A report "Adolescent Health"[104] published by the British Medical Association in December 2003 stated that the present generation of children and teenagers will turn into the most obese and infertile adults in the history of mankind.[105]

Sugar

Refined sugar is extremely immune-suppressing and is the first item that should be cut out of the diet of anyone suffering from chronic illness or wanting to avoid it. A suppressed immune system opens the door to every serious disease, including cancer. Caffeine exacerbates this effect.[106]

Hydrogenated Vegetable Oil

For decades, the public health authorities persuaded the public that animal fats were bad and that they should consume healthier poly-unsaturated fats found in vegetable oils. The current hysteria regarding cholesterol stems from research done during the 1940s and 1950s by the manufacturers of the new margarines and "healthy" fats made with hydrogenated vegetable oils. The suggestion was that choles-terol (specifically, LDL cholesterol) was responsible for heart disease, which was even then beginning to increase due to the relatively high-fat diet enjoyed by most westerners. This is not borne out by the facts. Western diets had always contained a relatively high proportion of red meat. In 1978, Dr. Mary Enig also proved that cancer rates were directly related to consumption of vegetable oils (including hydro-

104. image.guardian.co.uk/sys-files/Society/documents/2003/12/08/BMA_Adoles-centHealth.pdf

105. "Today's teens becoming world's sickest adults." WND, 9 Dec. 2003. www.wnd.com/2003/12/22206/

106. Garth Nicolson and Richard Ngwenya, "Dietary Considerations for Patients with Chronic Illnesses and Multiple Chronic Infections: A Brief Outline of Eighteen Dietary Steps to Better Health." Towsend Lett. Doctors, 2001; 219:62-65. www.immed.org/illness/treatment_considerations.html

genated vegetable oils) and total fat intake, but not related to animal fat consumption. This research is often ignored by the cholesterol lobby despite the fact that it has been confirmed by other researchers. When food manufacturers heat vegetable oil at very high temperatures (250–400°C), and usually in the presence of catalysts, they undergo hydrogenation which turns them into saturated fats. The melting point of the oil is raised, turning many previously liquid oils into solids. Shelf life is increased as the resulting oil is less susceptible to degrading over time. All nutritional value in the original oil is lost. The texture of the resultant solid can be made to resemble that of natural animal fats. However, during this process, trans fats are formed, which are found to cause significant increases in blood cholesterol. Most processed foods in supermarkets that contain fat will therefore be laden with these potentially lethal trans fats.[107]

Ischaemic heart disease (IHD) was virtually unknown until the 1940s, when hydrogenated vegetable oils were introduced. Now it is one of the biggest killers in the Western world. The dangers of trans fats were recognized as long ago as 1958, but the vegetable oil industry continues to badmouth safer natural animal fats.

Excitotoxins

There are a growing number of clinicians and scientists who are convinced that a group of compounds called excitotoxins play a critical role in the development of several neurological disorders. *Excitotoxins: The Taste That Kills,* by neurosurgeon Dr. Russell Blaylock,[108] describes how the common flavor enhancers monosodium glutamate, hydrolyzed vegetable protein, and aspartame/NutraSweet are extremely neurotoxic. They literally put holes in the brain and cause neurological diseases and cancer, as proven in an enormous body of scientific research. Brain tumors grow rapidly in the presence of the concentration of glutamic acid. Fully aware of these facts, the pub-

---

107. "Dangers of Trans Fats." Dr. Mary Enig interviewed by Richard A. Passwater, PHD, at: articles.mercola.com/sites/articles/archive/2000/06/10/trans-fats.aspx
108. Russell L. Blaylock. *Excitotoxins: The Taste That Kills.* Health Press, 1996.

lic health regulators have allowed hundreds of millions of people to consume excitotoxins for over fifty years.

The sweetener aspartame would never have been approved by the u.s. Food and Drug Administration in 1981 without lobbying by G. D. Searle & Co. (since bought out by Monsanto), headed by Donald Rumsfeld. The FDA regulators who approved aspartame went on to take jobs in the multibillion dollar aspartame industry. In addition to the FDA Commissioner who left to take up a job with G. D. Searle, four other FDA officials connected with the approval of aspartame took positions connected with the aspartame industry between 1979 and 1982: the Deputy FDA Commissioner, the Special Assistant to the FDA Commissioner, the Associate Director of the Bureau of Foods and Toxicology, and the attorney involved with the Public Board of Inquiry.[109]

The FDA once listed 92 adverse reactions from 10,000 consumer complaints and would send the list to all inquirers. In 1996, the FDA stopped taking complaints and now denies existence of the report.

Worse still, regulations allow food manufacturers to label their foods "contains no flavor enhancers" if the MSG content is less than 99% pure. MSG can be described as anything the food companies like, such as "spice extracts" or "natural flavorings."[110] Most savoury processed foods purchased in supermarkets contain either MSG or hydrolyzed vegetable protein.

Soy

In 1924, soybean production in the u.s. was only at 1.8 million acres harvested. Today, the soybean is America's third largest crop (harvesting 72 million acres in 1998), supplying more than 50% of the world's soybean demand. Most of these beans are made into animal feed and are manufactured into soy oil for use as vegetable oil, margarine, and shortening. For more than 20 years now, the soy industry has concentrated on finding alternative uses and new markets for soybeans and

---

109. Dr. Joseph Mercola. "Aspartame: What You Don't Know Can Hurt You." www.mercola.com/article/aspartame/fda.htm
110. www.truthinlabeling.org. See also in: Dr. Russell Blaylock, *op. cit.*

soy byproducts. It can now be found disguised as everything from soy cheese, milk, burgers, and hot dogs, to ice cream, yogurt, vegetable oil, baby formula, and flour. These are often marketed as low-fat, dairy-free, or as a high-protein meat substitute for vegetarians. But soy isn't always mentioned on food labels. Today, 60% of the food on America's supermarket shelves contain soy derivatives (i.e., soy flour, textured vegetable protein, partially hydrogenated soy bean oil, soy protein isolate).[111]

All soybean producers pay a mandatory assessment of one-half to one percent of the net market price of soybeans. The total—something like $80 million annually—supports United Soybean's program to strengthen the position of soybeans in the marketplace. Public relations firms help convert research projects into newspaper articles and advertising copy, and law firms lobby for favorable government regulations. IMF money funds soy processing plants in foreign countries, and free trade policies keep soybean abundance flowing to overseas destinations. The push for more soy consumption has been relentless and global in its reach.[112]

In October 1999, the U.S. Food and Drug Administration decided to allow a health claim for products "low in saturated fat and cholesterol" that contain 6.25 grams of soy protein per serving. The best marketing strategy for a product that is inherently unhealthy is, of course, a health claim.

Two senior U.S. government scientists, Drs. Daniel Doerge and Daniel Sheehan of the National Center for Toxicological Research, broke ranks with the FDA, claiming that soy could increase the risk of breast cancer in women, cause brain damage and thyroid disorders, and cause sexual abnormalities in infants. They wrote an internal protest letter warning of 28 studies revealing toxic effects of soy, mostly focusing on chemicals in soy known as isoflavones which have

---

111. Brandon Finucan & Charlotte Gerson, "Soy: Too Good to be True." *Gerson Institute Newsletter*, Volume 14, #3. articles.mercola.com/sites/articles/archive/2000/02/13/more-on-soy.aspx
112. Sally Fallon & Mary G. Enig, PHD. "Newest Research on Why You Should Avoid Soy." www.mercola.com/article/soy/avoid_soy.htm

effects similar to the female hormone oestrogen.[113] They pointed to a major study of 3,734 Japanese-American men, which found that soy consumption was associated with increased brain shrinkage in middle age, increased cognitive impairment and Alzheimer's disease.[114] Soy has the highest level of glutamic acid of any plant food, therefore, it has an excitotoxic effect on the brain.[115] In May 2003, the U.K. Government's Committee on Toxicity of Chemicals in Food, Consumer Products and the Environment issued a report on phytoestrogens and health. It concluded:

> After reviewing the data and conclusions in the report relating to soy-based infant formula, SACN [Scientific Advisory Committee on Nutrition] considered that there is cause for concern about the use of soy-based infant formula. Additionally, there is neither substantive medical need for nor health benefit arising from the use of soy-based infant formulae.

The Committee also noted that exposure to oestrogen in infants can lead to menstrual problems in females and low sperm count in males. "The amount of phytoestrogens that are in a day's worth of soy infant formula equals 5 birth control pills," says Mary G. Enig, PHD, president of the Maryland Nutritionists Association. She and other nutrition experts believe that infant exposure to high amounts of phytoestrogens is associated with early puberty in girls and retarded physical maturation in boys. A study published in *The Lancet* in July 1997, by Dr. K. Setchell et al, found that concentrations of soy isoflavones in the blood of infants tested were 13,000–22,000 times higher than natural oestrogen concentrations in early life.[116]

---

113. "Soy: Eating This "Healthy" Food? It Could Be Slowly and Silently Killing You," by The Weston A. Price Foundation. articles.mercola.com/sites/articles/archive/2010/12/04/soy-dangers-summarized.aspx
114. "Soy and Brain Damage," by John D. MacArthur. articles.mercola.com/sites/articles/archive/2000/09/17/soy-brain.aspx
115. Dr. Russell Blaylock, interviewed by Dr. Stanley Monteith on *Radio Liberty*, 2 December 2003. See: www.radioliberty.com
116. John D. MacArthur, *op. cit.*

A study of babies born to vegetarian mothers, published in the *British Journal of Urology* in January 2000, indicated just what those changes in baby's development might be. Mothers who ate a vegetarian diet during pregnancy had a fivefold greater risk of delivering a boy with hypospadias, a birth defect of the penis. The authors of the study suggested that the cause was greater exposure to phytoestrogens in soy foods popular with vegetarians.[117] Early maturation in girls is frequently a harbinger for problems with the reproductive system later in life, including failure to menstruate, infertility, and breast cancer.[118]

In short, soy is certainly nature's contraceptive and may also be affecting the sexual characteristics and sexual orientation of future generations. It is recognized that transsexuality is a medical condition caused by the effect of hormonal aberrations on the brain of the developing foetus. On 20 January 2005, the U.K. Civil Service website on Diversity reported:

> Estimates vary on the number of transvestite men in the population, owing to the lack of any research data whatsoever. Informed guesses have been as high as 1 in 20 adult males. Certainly, estimates between 1/100 and 1/200 would not be outrageous if judged only by the commercial success of businesses catering for the interests of those people. … Depending where you draw the line in what to count, between 1 in 200 and 1 in 1000 children are born with a visible or concealed ambiguity in their genitals, gonads and/or chromosomes which qualify them as intersex.

Soy is not the only substance linked to sexual changes in humans. *The National Geographic* magazine reported that scientists are warning that chemicals in pesticides, plastics and other products are "endocrine disrupters," which are having a serious gender-altering impact on both animals and humans.[119]

117. Sally Fallon & Mary G. Enig, *op. cit.*
118. *Ibid.*
119. James Owen, "Animals' Sexual Changes Linked to Waste, Chemicals." *National Geographic News*, 1 March 2004. news.nationalgeographic.com/news/2004/03/0301_040301_genderbender.html

Fluoride

Water fluoridation has been rejected by most Western European nations, but the U.K. currently fluoridates 11% of its water supply, and the U.S. around 60%. The 2003 Water Act requires British water companies to fluoridate the water supply if requested to do so by the local Strategic Health Authorities. However, any decision by health authorities must follow public consultation at the local level.[120]

A by-product of the nuclear power, fertilizer and other heavy industries, *fluoride is more toxic than lead and only marginally less toxic than arsenic.* Dr. R. Swinburne Clymer tried to expose the purpose of water fluoridation in his book, *The Age of Treason* (1957). He wrote:

> Charles Eliot Perkins, a research worker in chemistry, biochemistry, physiology and pathology ... was sent by the United States Government to help take charge of the IG Farben chemical plants in Germany at the end of the Second World War. What follows are statements from a letter which Mr. Perkins wrote the Lee Foundation for Nutritional Research...
>
> "... In the 1930s, Hitler and the German Nazis envisioned a world to be dominated and controlled by the Nazi philosophy of pan-Germanism. ... The German chemists worked out a very ingenious and far-reaching plan of mass control which was submitted to and adopted by the German General Staff. This plan was to control the population in any given area through mass medication of drinking water supplies. By this method, they could control the population of whole areas, reduce population by water medication that would produce sterility in the women, and so on. In this scheme of mass control, *sodium fluoride* occupied a prominent place.
>
> We are told by the ideologists who are advocating the *fluoridation of water supplies* in this country that their purpose is to reduce the incidence of tooth decay in children... The real reason behind *flu-*

---

120. Debbie Andalo. "Public to make fluoride decision." *The Guardian*, 28 July 2004. fluoridealert.org/news/public-to-make-fluoride-decision/. See also: Andy Kelly, "We'll Fight Fluoride Tooth and Nail, Warns Council." *Daily Post,* 2 August 2004. fluoridealert.org/news/well-fight-fluoride-tooth-and-nail-warns-council/

orination is not to benefit children's teeth. The real purpose behind water *fluorination* is to reduce the resistance of the masses to domination and control and loss of liberty. … There is a small area of brain tissue that is responsible for the individual's power to resist domination. Repeated doses of infinitesimal amounts of fluorine will in time gradually reduce the individual's power to resist domination by slowly poisoning and narcotizing this area of brain tissue and make him submissive to the will of those who wish to govern him.

… Any person who drinks artificially *fluorinated* water for a period of one year or more will never again be the same person, mentally or physically."[121] [Emphases added.]

On 29th June 2000, Dr. William J. Hirzy testified before the U.S. Senate Subcommittee on Wildlife, Fisheries and Drinking Water.[122] He represented the labour union of the professional toxicologists, biologists, chemists, engineers and lawyers working at the headquarters of the U.S. Environmental Protection Agency (EPA). The union voted to oppose water fluoridation in 1997. These are some of the points Dr. Hirzy made to the committee:

- According to a study by the National Institute of Dental Research, 66% of American children in fluoridated communities show the visible sign of overexposure and fluoride toxicity, dental fluorosis.
- In 1998, the results of a fifty-year fluoridation experiment involving Kingston, NY (non-fluoridated), and Newburg, NY (fluoridated), were published. In summary, there is no overall significant difference in rates of dental decay in children in the two cities, but children in the fluoridated city show significantly higher rates of dental fluorosis than children in the non-fluoridated city.
- There is epidemiological evidence of elevated bone cancer in young men related to consumption of fluoridated drinking water.
- In 1990, the results of the National Toxicology Program (NTP)

---

121. Stanley Monteith, MD. *Radio Liberty Newsletter.* November, 2004. www.radio-liberty.com/nlnov04.html
122. *Fluoride Alert.* fluoridealert.org/fan-tv/hirzy/

cancer bioassay on sodium fluoride were published, the initial findings of which would have ended fluoridation. But a special commission was hastily convened to review the findings, resulting in the salvation of fluoridation through systematic downgrading of the evidence of carcinogenicity. The final, published version of the NTP report says that there is "equivocal evidence of carcinogenicity in male rats," changed from "clear evidence of carcinogenicity in male rats." The change prompted Dr. William Marcus, who was then Senior Science Adviser and Toxicologist in the Office of Drinking Water, to blow the whistle about the issue, which led to his firing by EPA. Dr. Marcus sued EPA, won his case, and was reinstated with back pay, benefits and compensatory damages.

- Since 1994 there have been six publications that link fluoride exposure to direct adverse effects on the brain. Two epidemiology studies from China indicate depression of IQ in children. A 1998 paper shows brain and kidney damage in animals given the "optimal" dosage of fluoride, viz. one part per million. Another publication links fluoride dosing to adverse effects on the brains pineal gland and premature onset of sexual maturity in animals.

- In three landmark cases adjudicated since 1978 in Pennsylvania, Illinois and Texas, judges with no interest except finding fact and administering justice, heard prolonged testimony from proponents and opponents of fluoridation. None of them could find evidence supporting fluoridation but all were convinced of its toxicity. Judge Anthony Farris in Texas found that "the artificial fluoridation of public water supplies, such as contemplated by [Houston] City ordinance No. 80-2530, may cause or contribute to the cause of cancer, genetic damage, intolerant reactions, and chronic toxicity, including dental mottling, in man; that the said artificial fluoridation may aggravate malnutrition and existing illness in man; and that the value of said artificial fluoridation is in some doubt as to reduction of tooth decay in man.

- In recent years, two prominent dental researchers who were leaders of the pro-fluoridation movement announced reversals

of their former positions because they concluded that water fluoridation is not an effective means of reducing dental caries and
that it poses serious risks to human health. The late Dr. John Col-
quhoun was Principal Dental Officer of Aukland, New Zealand,
and he published his reasons for changing sides in 1997. In 1999,
Dr. Hardy Limeback, Head of Preventive Dentistry, University of
Toronto, announced his change of views, then published a statement dated April 2000.

The scientific literature is full of studies that support Dr. Hirzy's testimony. Animal studies show decreased fertility and higher rates of
miscarriage in animals that drank fluoridated water. Fluoridation
leads to osteoporosis and increased fractures. Regions with high levels of fluoride in the drinking water have 220% more fractures. Fluoride accumulates in the thyroid gland and produces hypothyroid-
ism. Communities with fluoridated water have higher rates of cancer
than non-fluoridated communities. The incidence of osteogenic sarcoma in males is 70% higher in fluoridated regions. Phyllis Mulle-
nix showed the disastrous effect of water fluoridation on the brains
of unborn and newborn animals, and numerous studies show a reduction of IQ in humans. Fluoride is the active ingredient in Prozac,
Paxil, and several other widely used psychotrophic medications.[123]

The U.S. Food and Drug Administration has never approved any
fluoride product for the purpose of preventing tooth decay.

Germ Warfare

AIDS

"In the event that I am reincarnated, I would like to return as a deadly
virus, in order to contribute something to solve overpopulation."
—Attributed to HRH Prince Philip.

By 2020, UNAIDS estimates seventy million people will have died
from AIDS.[124] There is scientific controversy over what causes AIDS.

123. Stanley Monteith. *Radio Liberty Newsletter*. Nov. 2004. www.radioliberty.com
124. "China, India face AIDS disaster." *BBC News*, 3 July 2003. news.bbc.co.uk

Not all researchers agree that the HIV virus causes AIDS. Some believe that AIDS is caused by the toxic drugs such as AZT used to treat the infection or is a cumulative result of malnutrition and other environmental and lifestyle factors.

However, it wasn't long after AIDS appeared in the early 1980s that rumors of its man-made origins began to circulate. Most doctors will dismiss this as lunacy, but both the National Institutes of Health and Rockefellers' Exxon Mobil subscribe to a publication dedicated to the idea—the *Journal of Degenerative Diseases*. I have subscribed to the journal since 2001, and am member of the Common Cause Medical Foundation, which publishes it. The Foundation was set up by a retired Canadian professor named Donald Scott. He began researching chronic fatigue syndrome (CFS)/myalgic encephalomyelitis (ME), but over a number of years he came to the conclusion that a whole range of chronic diseases had a common cause and that this was most likely a biological warfare agent developed by the U.S. military.

Much of the groundwork had already been prepared, not least by the book *Emerging Viruses: AIDS and Ebola*, published in 1996. Harvard Public Health graduate and practicing dentist, Dr. Leonard Horowitz documented how AIDS was manufactured in the laboratories of American universities and U.S. military biological warfare contractors during the 1960s and 70s. The program was secret until 1972, when it was publicly named the "War on Cancer."

Dr. Horowitz's research confirmed the ideas of Californian pharmacologist, Dr. Robert Strecker. In his film produced in the late 1980s, *The Strecker Memorandum*, Dr. Strecker states that HIV is genomically very similar to the visna virus of sheep and the bovine leukemia virus of cattle, and that this hybrid could have been created in the laboratory. The documents discovered by Horowitz showed that the National Cancer Institute's Special Virus Cancer Program 1964–1978 (SVCP; called Special Virus Leukemia Program until 1968) involved recombining animal immunodeficiency viruses and cancer viruses. Self-proclaimed co-discoverer of HIV, Dr. Bob Gallo, was a senior SVCP scientist.

Most of the SVCP reports were shredded during the Watergate scandal, but many surviving copies of the 15 annual progress reports have been retrieved. Horowitz concluded that HIV was introduced to gay males in the U.S. and into blacks in Africa in the late 1970s through experimental vaccine programs, in particular, the hepatitis B vaccine developed by Merck Sharpe & Dohm, Inc. *Emerging Viruses* contains an endorsement from Dr. Garth Nicolson, one of the world's leading microbiologists and researchers on Gulf War Illness and former consultant to the U.S. Department of Defense:

> One cannot fail to grasp the explosive significance of this book and its main thesis that biological weapons programs developed and field-tested immune-system-destroying agents that now cannot be contained.

Dr. John Martin, a former Food and Drug Administration insider and expert on the cover-up of animal virus contamination of human polio vaccines, wrote the foreword to the book.

However, *Emerging Viruses* did not address the key question posed by the AIDS dissidents such as Dr. Peter Duesberg: Does HIV really cause AIDS? Donald Scott's research into the symptoms of CFS, AIDS, and other neuro-systemic diseases, suggests that they are consistent with chronic mycoplasma infection, a strain of tiny bacteria. Until quite recently, most doctors hadn't heard of mycoplasma even though it is documented in the scientific literature going back a hundred years. Mycoplasma fermentans was identified by IG Farben during WWII and was one of the biological agents tested on prisoners in the concentration camps.

Disabling Agents

Whilst AIDS is depopulating the Third World, the West is being plagued by a multitude of disabling diseases. Disease is an important tool for maintaining the social hierarchy by two methods: firstly, by making people dependent upon the petrochemical cartel for treatment, and secondly, by reducing living standards. Certain disabling diseases, in which mycoplasma infection plays a significant role, appeared in the West at the same time as AIDS. These include CFS or Myalgic encephalomyelitis (ME), fibromyalgia, and Lyme disease.

Even based on the public health authorities' very conservative es-
timate of 0.4% prevalence, CFS/ME has disabled over a million Americans and 250,000 British. The true figures are possibly double these.
No specific pharmaceutical treatment is being developed, and there
has been a coordinated effort by the health authorities in the West to
deny this disease even exists and then to label it a psychiatric disorder despite the overwhelming evidence of an infectious origin. Many
independent researchers have come up with inexpensive, proven,
and effective treatment regimes, but the health authorities refuse to
recognize them.

The cover-up was documented in *Osier's Web*, a book written in
1996 by Hillary Johnson, a former *Wall Street Journal* writer and *Life*
staff reporter. Ms Johnson has since disappeared and the publishers
are "no longer allowed" to print this book.[125] The same public health
policy is being applied to Lyme disease, which is very similar to CFS/
ME. Even though it is recognized as being an infectious disease, the
authorities are blocking doctors from using inexpensive long-term
antibiotic treatment, which is proven to be effective.

The CIA press release, entitled "The Darker Bioweapons Future,"
confirmed the viability of biological agents for economic warfare. It
reports that a panel of experts from the National Academy of Sciences
studying the future threat of biological weapons believed that a genetically engineered stealth virus could be used to cripple a large number
of people in their forties and fifties with severe arthritis, concealing
its hostile origin and leaving a country with massive health and economic problems. It also warned that, "the effects of these engineered
biological agents could be worse than any disease known to man" and
that advances in biotechnology will be very hard to police.[126]

Coming Plagues

"Rebuilding America's Defenses," written in September 2000 by the
neoconservative think-tank, Project for the New American Century

125. Hillary Johnson, *Osier's Web*. New York: Crown Publishers, Inc., 1996.
126. "The Darker Bioweapons Future." The CIA Press Release (ref. OTI SF 2003-108).
     fas.org/irp/cia/product/bw1103.pdf

(PNAC), hints that the U.S. may consider developing biological weapons "that can target specific genotypes [and] may transform biological warfare from the realm of terror to a politically useful tool."[127]

Depleted Uranium

Depleted uranium is a serious health hazard, when DU munitions are fired and burn up on impact. Radioactive dust blows around in the air, enabling the DU to get into the body through the lungs and broken skin.

On behalf of the U.S. Army, Major Doug Rokke led a 434-man depleted uranium clean-up team in the first Gulf War. The entire team became sick from DU exposure almost as soon as they arrived in the Gulf. In 1994, he was appointed as depleted uranium project director for the U.S. Army. Despite his warnings of the dangers of DU exposure, both the U.S. Army and coalition forces continued to use DU munitions with catastrophic effects on both their own troops and civilian populations.

Dr. Rokke and many other researchers believe that the hundreds of tonnes of DU dust deposited in Iraq, Afghanistan and the former Yugoslavia are responsible for an epidemic of cancers, birth defects and an array of neuro-systemic degenerative diseases in both Allied troops and native populations. This is, in fact, a covert form of nuclear warfare, the effects of which may never properly be known.

Forced Abortion and Sterilization

Thirty million women a year are forced to undergo abortion or sterilization in China. Leading Chinese dissident and Executive Director of Laogai Research Foundation Harry Wu states that the United Nations Population Fund (UNFPA) cooperates closely with the Chinese government in implementing the one child policy. An independent Population Research Institute (PRI) studied a UNFPA's so-called "model county" program in China between 27–30 September 2001. It found that "voluntary" family planning in the Sihui County UNFPA program

127. Michael Meacher, "This war on terrorism is bogus." *The Guardian*, 6 September 2003. www.theguardian.com/politics/2003/sep/06/september11.iraq

did not exist. The team was told by Chinese Family Planning officials that there was no distinction between UNFPA's work in this county and their own. Chinese officials showed the UNFPA office desk, which was located within the local Chinese Family Planning Office.[128]

Norplant is an implant which prevents pregnancy for at least five years. It can only be removed by surgery. The patent is held by the Rockefeller-funded Population Council. The BBC documentary, *Horizon: The Human Laboratory,* showed how these implants are not easily removed, and in many cases the doctors refuse to take them out, even if they are causing severe side effects. Despite this, it is being tested on tens of thousands of women around the world.

GM Food

The Ecologist magazine reported that adopting GM crops would place farmers and the food chain itself under the control of a handful of multinational corporations such as Monsanto, Syngenta, Bayer, and DuPont. For U.S. farmers, this has meant:

1) Legally-binding agreements that force farmers to purchase expensive new seeds from the biotech corporations each season.
2) Having to buy these corporations' herbicides (at a cost considerably above that of a generic equivalent) for herbicide-tolerant crops.
3) Paying the biotech firms a technology fee based on the acreage of land under GM.
4) The development of so-called "traitor technology" crops, on which particular chemicals will have to be applied if the crops' GM characteristics (such as their time of flowering or disease resistance) are to show.
5) The invention of "terminator technology" that stops GM plants producing fertile seeds; thus, farmers are physically prevented from sowing saved seed and have to buy new seed from the biotech firms instead.

128. Steven W. Mosher, Pres., PRI. "The Case Against UNFPA Funding." PRI Weekly Briefing, 11 Jan. 2002, Vol. 4/ No. 2. pop.org/content/case-against-unfpa-funding

6) Biotech firms buying up seed companies. This creates monopolies and limits farmers' choices still further. DuPont and Monsanto are now the two largest seed companies in the world. As a result of their control of the seed industry, farmers are reporting that good non-GM seed varieties are rapidly disappearing.

According to the U.K. Soil Association, "all non-GM farmers in North America are finding it very hard or impossible to grow GM-free crops. Seeds have become almost completely contaminated with GM organisms (GMO), good non-GM varieties have become hard to buy, and there is a high risk of crop contamination." The U.K. Government's official adviser on GM, the Agriculture and Environment Biotechnology Commission (AEBC), has said it would be "difficult and in some places impossible to guarantee" that any British food was GM-free, if commercial growing of GM crops went ahead. In North America, farmers can no longer be certain the seed they plant does not contain GM genes.[129]

GM food scientists can increase the vitamin content of food, so there is no reason why they cannot reduce it in order to increase malnutrition, disease, and death on a large scale. For example, more than $100 million has been spent over 10 years to produce transgenic rice at the Institute of Plant Sciences in Zurich. The Zurich team introduced three genes taken from daffodils and bacteria into a rice strain to produce a yellow rice with high levels of beta-carotene, which is converted to vitamin A within the body. As well as altering vitamin content, over 300 open-field trials of "pharma" crops have taken place around the world since 1991. In California, for example, GM rice containing human genes has been grown for drug production. Pharmaceutical wheat, corn and barley are also being developed in the U.S., France and Canada. A biotech company called Prodigene has been working on growing edible vaccines in corn and in November 2000 began trials on an edible AIDS vaccine.

By introducing drugs into food, GM technology has huge population control potential.

_____

129. "5 reasons to keep Britain GM-free." *The Ecologist*, 22 June 2003.

Weather Modification Technology

Weather modification technology exists in America and Europe. The ability to deploy this technology for global depopulation without detection must be extremely tempting for the Malthusians since droughts, hurricanes, and floods can be blamed on natural weather variability, solar flares, and global warming. A study of future military strategy called "Airforce 2025" was drawn up by the U.S. Air University in 1996.[130] In the section entitled "Weather as a Force Multiplier: Owning the Weather in 2025," the authors state that altering weather patterns will eventually become an "integral part of U.S. national security policy with both domestic and international applications." By 2025, the Air Force fully expects to be able to influence the weather "on a mesoscale (<200 sq km) or microscale (immediate local area) to achieve operational capabilities… Achieving such a highly accurate and reasonably precise weather-modification capability in the next 30 years will require overcoming some challenging but not insurmountable technological and legal hurdles," the report said. "The lessons of history indicate a real weather-modification capability will eventually exist despite the risk [because] the drive exists. People have always wanted to control the weather and their desire will compel them to collectively and continuously pursue their goal," the report concluded. The military also aim to deny an enemy satellite communication capabilities by modifying the Earth's ionosphere.

One of the stated objectives of the U.S. Defense Department's High Frequency Active Auroral Research Program (HAARP) is to "simulate and control ionospheric processes that might alter the performance of communications and surveillance systems."[131] The HAARP Ionospheric Research Facility was established in Gakona, Alaska, on 18th October 1993. HAARP can beam 3.6 Gigawatts of high frequency radio energy from earth-based antennae into the ionosphere.[132] According to the HAARP website factsheet,

130. "Airforce 2025." The Air University website: www.au.af.mil/au/2025/

131. "Purpose and Objectives of the HAARP Program as Stated in the Environmental Impact Statement." HAARP website: www.haarp.alaska.edu/haarp/prpeis.html

132. Rosalie Bertell, PHD. "GNSH, Background of the HAARP Project." *Earth Pulse* website: www.earthpulse.com/src/subcategory.asp?catid=1&subcatid=1

Interest in the ionosphere is not limited to the U.S.: a five-country consortium operates the European Incoherent Scatter Radar site (EISCAT), a premier world-class ionospheric research facility located in northern Norway, near Tromso. Facilities are also located at Jicamarca, Peru; near Moscow, Nizhny Novgorod (SURA), and Apatity, Russia; near Kharkov, Ukraine, and in Dushanbe, Tadzhikistan.[133]

"Airforce 2025" does not specify HAARP as a weather modification device, and it is not one of the HAARP's official purposes. However, the U.S. patent on HAARP's technology states that it can serve as a giant ionospheric heater:

> In such experiments, certain regions of the ionosphere are heated to change the electron density and temperature within these regions. This is accomplished by transmitting from earth-based antennae high frequency electromagnetic radiation at a substantial angle to, not parallel to, the ionosphere's magnetic field to heat the ionospheric particles primarily by ohmic heating. The electron temperature of the ionosphere has been raised by hundreds of degrees in these experiments, and electrons with several electron volts of energy have been produced in numbers sufficient to enhance airglow.[134]

The disclosure section of the patent adds:

> The production of enhanced ionization will also alter the distribution of atomic and molecular constituents of the atmosphere, most notably through increased atomic nitrogen concentration. The upper atmosphere is normally rich in atomic oxygen (the dominant atmospheric constituent above 200 km altitude), but atomic nitrogen is normally relatively rare. This can be expected to manifest itself in

---

133. HAARP Factsheet: www.haarp.alaska.edu/haarp/haarpFactSheet.html
134. "Background Art, Method and Apparatus for Altering a Region in the Earth's Atmosphere, Ionosphere, and/or Magnetosphere." U.S. patent No. 4,686,605; 11 August 1987. Go to http://www.uspto.gov/patft/index.html and type in the patent number. The patent is held by Advanced Power Technologies, formerly ARCO Power Technologies, a division of the Atlantic Richfield Oil Company.

increased air glow, among other effects… This invention has a phenomenal variety of possible ramifications and potential future developments. As alluded to earlier, missile or aircraft destruction, deflection, or confusion could result, particularly when relativistic particles are employed. Also, large regions of the atmosphere could be lifted to an unexpectedly high altitude so that missiles encounter unexpected and unplanned drag forces with resultant destruction or deflection of same. *Weather modification* [emphasis added] is possible by, for example, altering upper atmosphere wind patterns or altering solar absorption patterns by constructing one or more plumes of atmospheric particles which will act as a lens or focusing device.

HAARP is clearly one of the weather modification technologies known to the authors of "2025."

The world's foremost independent investigator of HAARP is Dr. Nick Begich from Alaska, the author of the book *Angels Don't Play This HAARP*.[135] He explains:

HAARP zaps the ionosphere where it is relatively unstable. A point to remember is that the ionosphere is an active electrical shield protecting the planet from the constant bombardment of high-energy particles from space. This conducting plasma, along with Earth's magnetic field, traps the electrical plasma of space and holds it back from going directly to the Earth's surface, says Charles Yost of Dynamic Systems, Leicester, North Carolina. "If the ionosphere is greatly disturbed, the atmosphere below is subsequently disturbed."[136]

Dr. Begich also considers the role of weather modification as a weapon of mass destruction:

In 1966, Professor Gordon J. F. MacDonald was associate director of

---

135. Nick Begich and Jeane Manning. *Angels Don't Play This HAARP: Advances in Tesla Technology*. Earthpulse, 1995.
136. Dr. Nick Begich and Jeane Manning, "Vandalism In The Sky." *Earth Pulse* website: www.earthpulse.com/src/subcategory.asp?catid=1&subcatid=2

the Institute of Geophysics and Planetary Physics at the University of California, Los Angeles, was a member of the President's Science Advisory Committee, and later a member of the President's Council on Environmental Quality. He published papers on the use of environmental control technologies for military purposes. MacDonald made a revealing comment: "The key to geophysical warfare is the identification of environmental instabilities to which the addition of a small amount of energy would release vastly greater amounts of energy." MacDonald had a number of ideas for using the environment as a weapon system and he contributed to what was, at the time, the dream of a futurist. When he wrote his chapter, "How to Wreck the Environment," for the book *Unless Peace Comes*,[137] he was not kidding around. In it he describes the use of weather manipulation, climate modification, polar ice cap melting or destabilization, ozone depletion techniques, earthquake engineering, ocean wave control and brain wave manipulation using the planet's energy fields. He also said that these types of weapons would be developed and, when used, would be virtually undetectable by their victims.

It is worth noting that this book was written two years after the *Report From Iron Mountain*. This report identified environmental disaster as a credible substitute for war for the purpose of preserving social hierarchy once world government had established permanent peace.

In response to Dr. Nick Begich's 6th February 1998 testimony to the European Parliament's Foreign Affairs Subcommittee on Security and Disarmament in Brussels, Swedish MEP, Mrs. Maj Britt Theorin, put forward a motion for an independent international inquiry into HAARP a year later. The resolution describes HAARP as a weapons system, which disrupts the climate and, "by virtue of its far-reaching impact on the environment to be a global concern, calls for its legal, ecological and ethical implications to be examined by an international independent body before any further research and testing; regrets the repeated refusal of the U.S. Administration to send anyone

---

137. *Unless Peace Comes: A Scientific Forecast of New Weapons.* New York: Viking Press, 1968.

in person to give evidence to the public hearing or any subsequent meeting held by its competent committee into the environmental and public risks connected with the HAARP program currently being funded in Alaska…"[138]

Eugenics: The Final Solution

The foundations for the genetic manipulation of humankind envisioned in Aldous Huxley's *Brave New World* have already been laid.

Biological Warfare

"Rebuilding America's Defenses" by the American think-tank PNAC states that race-specific bioweapons could be a "politically useful tool." Furthermore, the epidemiology of the global AIDS pandemic indicates that the population control agenda does have a bias against blacks. 70% of the world's 42 million AIDS cases are in sub-Saharan Africa. Africa makes up only 14% of the world's population. 40% of American AIDS victims are black; blacks make up only 13% of the American population.[139]

Cloning

A cloned human embryo does not result from the random union of sperm and egg, but from a process called somatic cell nuclear transfer, in which the nucleus containing DNA from a cell of one individual is put into an egg whose nucleus has been removed. The resulting cloned embryo becomes virtually genetically identical to the individual whose DNA was inserted into the enucleated egg.

In September 2003, it had been reported that at the University of Kentucky the first cloned human embryo was ready to be implanted into a surrogate mother for the purpose of cloning children.[140]

---

138. Report of the European Parliament Committee on Foreign Affairs, Security and Defense Policy. Minutes of 14 Jan. 1999, Section 24, ref. A4-0005/1999.

139. World HIV and AIDS statistics: www.avert.org/worldwide-hiv-aids-statistics.htm

140. Andy Coghlan, "First human clone embryo ready for implantation." *New Scientist,* 15 September 2003. www.newscientist.com/article/dn4168-first-human-clone-embryo-ready-for-implantation.html

Euthanasia

Polls show that most people favour assisted suicide, believing in the right to die with dignity. However, other side of the coin is that the elite want the right to terminate us and to legalize euthanasia for this purpose. In December 1999, a senior consultant at a London hospital voiced concern that there was a policy of "involuntary euthanasia" by depriving elderly patients of food and water.[141] The British charity Age Concern states that there is a policy of not resuscitating seriously ill elderly patients.[142] The chilling exposé of euthanasia in the United States, *Forced Exit* by Wesley J. Smith reveals how people entering hospital sign "living wills" allowing the hospital not to resuscitate them, if they fall into a coma, only to find they are used by the hospital to deny patients treatment.[143] In the U.K., doctors can and do put "Do not resuscitate" on patients medical records without their consent.[144]

The Human Genome Project

Some of the work on the Human Genome Project is being done at the Cold Spring Harbor Laboratory, NY. This was the old Station for Experimental Evolution and the Eugenics Records office and was endowed with funds from the Rockefeller and Harriman families in 1910. It was dedicated to scientific research of racial differences. Like the RIIA (Royal Institute of International Affairs), the Bilderberg Group, the CFR (Counsil on Foreign Relations), and Trilateral Commission, the Cold Spring Harbor Laboratory host secret conferences. Its Banbury Center meetings are off-the-record discussions on molecular biology and genetics, human genetics, and science policy by the world's leading scientists.[145]

*   *   *

141. "NHS euthanasia claims 'ludicrous." *BBC News*, 6 December 1999. news.bbc.co.uk
142. "Curb doctors' life or death powers." *BBC News*, 28 April 2000. news.bbc.co.uk
143. Wesley J. Smith. *Forced Exit*. Times Books, 1997.
144. "Patients must decide on resuscitation." *BBC News*, 27 June 2000. news.bbc. co.uk/2/hi/health/808206.stm
145. Cold Spring Harbor Laboratory: www.cshl.org/Banbury/Organization.html

Alongside the physical science of genetic engineering emerged the social science of "bioethics", the discipline which decides what is ethical medical practice and research.

UNESCO established an International Bioethics Committee in 1993. What used to be called genocide will masquerade as *"social engineering"* administered by pseudoscientific committees. In matters of life and death, the ruling elite still has the final word.

Updated excerpt from issue 9 of The Dot Connector Magazine
(May-June 2010).

The Drug Story
The Truth About the Rockefeller Drug Empire

By Hans Ruesch (1913–2007)

In the 1930s, Morris A. Bealle, a former city editor of the old *Washington Times* and *Herald*, was running a county seat newspaper, in which the local power company bought a large advertisement every week. This account took quite a lot of worry off Bealle's shoulders when the bills came due. But according to Bealle's own story, one day the paper took up the cudgels for some of its readers that were being given poor service from the power company, and Morris Bealle received the dressing down of his life from the advertising agency which handled the power company's account. They told him that any more such "stepping out of line" would result in the immediate cancellation of the advertising contract not only with the power company, but also with the gas company and the telephone company.

That's when Bealle's eyes were opened to the meaning of a "free press," and he decided to get out of the newspaper business. He could afford to do that because he belonged to the landed gentry of Maryland, but not all newspaper editors are that lucky. Bealle used his professional experience to do some deep digging into the freedom of the press situation and came up with two shattering exposés—*The Drug Story* (1949) and *The House of Rockefeller* (1959). The fact that in spite of his familiarity with the editorial world and many important personal contacts he couldn't get his revelations into print until he founded his own company, The Columbia Publishing House, Washington, D.C., in 1949, was just a prime example of the silent but adamant censorship in force in "the Land of the Free and the Home

149

of the Brave." Although *The Drug Story* is one of the most important books on health and politics ever to appear in the USA, it has never been admitted to a major bookstore nor reviewed by any establishment paper, and was sold exclusively by mail. Nevertheless, when we first got to read it, in the 1970s, it was already in its 33rd printing, under a different label—Biworld Publishers, Orem, Utah.

Examples

As Bealle pointed out, a business which makes 6% on its invested capital is considered a sound money maker. Sterling Drug, Inc., the largest holding company in the Rockefeller Drug Empire and its 68 subsidiaries, showed operating profits in 1961 of $23,463,719 after taxes, on net assets of $43,108,106—a 54% profit. Squibb, another Rockefeller-controlled company, in 1945 made not 6% but 576% on the actual value of its property. That was during the luscious war years when the Army Surgeon General's Office and the Navy Bureau of Medicine and Surgery were not only acting as promoters for the Drug Trust, but were actually forcing Drug Trust poisons into the bloodstreams of American soldiers, sailors and marines, to the tune of over 200 million "shots." Is it any wonder, asked Bealle, that the Rockefellers, and their stooges in the Food and Drug Administration, the U.S. Public Health Service, the Federal Trade Commission, the Better Business Bureau, the Army Medical Corps, the Navy Bureau of Medicine, and thousands of health officers all over the country, should combine to put out of business all forms of therapy that discourage the use of drugs.

"The last annual report of the Rockefeller Foundation," reported Bealle, "itemizes the gifts it has made to colleges and public agencies in the past 44 years, and they total somewhat over half a billion dollars. These colleges, of course, teach their students all the drug lore the Rockefeller pharmaceutical houses want taught. Otherwise there would be no more gifts, just as there are no gifts to any of the 30 odd colleges in the United States that don't use therapies based on drugs."

Harvard, with its well-publicized medical school, has received $8,764,433 of Rockefeller's Drug Trust money, Yale got $7,927,800,

Johns Hopkins $10,418,531,Washington University in St. Louis $2,842,132, Cornell University $1,709,072, New York's Columbia University $5,424,371, etc. And while "giving away" those huge sums to drug-propagandizing colleges, the Rockefeller interests were growing to a world-wide web that no one could entirely explore. Already well over 30 years ago it was large enough for Bealle to demonstrate that the Rockefeller interests had created, built up and developed the most far reaching industrial empire ever conceived in the mind of man. Standard Oil was of course the foundation upon which all of the other Rockefeller industries have been built. The story of Old John D., as ruthless an industrial pirate as ever came down the pike, is well known, but is being today conveniently ignored.

The keystone of this mammoth industrial empire was the Chase National Bank, now renamed the Chase Manhattan Bank. Not the least of its holdings are in the drug business. The Rockefellers own the largest drug manufacturing combine in the world, and use all of their other interests to bring pressure to increase the sale of drugs. The fact that most of the 12,000 separate drug items on the market are harmful is of no concern to the Drug Trust.

The Rockefeller Foundation

The Rockefeller Foundation was first set up in 1904 and called the General Education Fund. An organization called the Rockefeller Foundation, ostensibly to supplement the General Education Fund, was formed in 1910 and through long finagling and lots of Rockefeller money got the New York legislature to issue a charter on May 14, 1913. It is therefore not surprising that the House of Rockefeller has had its own "nominees" planted in all Federal agencies that have to do with health. So the stage was set for the "education" of the American public, with a view to turning it into a population of drug and medico dependents, with the early help of the parents and the schools, then with direct advertising and, last but not least, the influence the advertising revenues had on the media-makers.

A compilation of the magazine *Advertising Age* showed that as far back as 1948 the larger companies in America spent for advertising the sum total of $1,104,224,374, when the dollar was still worth a dollar and not half a zloty. Of this staggering sum the interlocking Rockefeller-Morgan interests (gone over entirely to Rockefeller after Morgan's death) controlled about 80 percent, and utilized it to manipulate public information on health and drug matters—then and even more recklessly now.

Censorship

"Even the most independent newspapers are dependent on their press associations for their national news," Bealle pointed out, "and there is no reason for a news editor to suspect that a story coming over the wires of the Associated Press, the United Press or the International News Service is censored when it concerns health matters. Yet this is what happens constantly."

In fact in the 1950s the Drug Trust had one of its directors on the directorate of the Associated Press. He was no less than Arthur Hays Sulzberger, publisher of the *New York Times* and as such one of the most powerful Associated Press directors. It was thus easy for the Rockefeller Trust to persuade the Associated Press Science Editor to adopt a policy which would not permit any medical news to clear that is not approved by the Drug Trust "expert," and this censor is not going to approve any item that can in any way hurt the sale of drugs. This accounts to this day for the many fake stories of serums and medical cures and just-around-the-corner breakthrough victories over cancer, AIDS, diabetes, multiple sclerosis, which go out brazenly over the wires to all daily newspapers in America and abroad.

Emanuel M. Josephson, MD, whom the Drug Trust has been unable to intimidate despite many attempts, pointed out that the National Association of Science Writers was "persuaded" to adopt as part of its code of ethics the following chestnut: "Science editors are incapable of judging the facts of phenomena involved in medical and scientific discovery. Therefore, they only report 'discoveries' approved by medical authorities…"

This explains why Bantam Books, America's biggest publisher, made a colossal mistake in its initial enthusiasm and optimism sending review copies of *Slaughter of the Innocent* to the 3,500 "science writers" on its list, instead of addressing them to the literary book reviewers who are not subject to medical censorship. One single censor decreed no and *Slaughter of the Innocent* sank in silence. Thus newspapers continue to be fed with propaganda about drugs and their alleged value, although according to the Food and Drug Administration (FDA) 1.5 million people landed in hospitals in 1978 because of medication side effects in the U.S. alone, and despite recurrent statements by intelligent and courageous medical men that most pharmaceutical items on sale are useless at best, but more often harmful or deadly in the long run.

The truth about cures without drugs is suppressed, unless it suits the purpose of the censor to garble it. Whether these cures are effected by Chiropractors, Naturopaths, Naprapaths, Osteopaths, Faith Healers, Spiritualists, Herbalists, Christian Scientists, or MDs who use the brains they have, you never read about it in the big newspapers. To teach the Rockefeller drug ideology, it is necessary to teach that Nature didn't know what she was doing when she made the human body. But statistics issued by the Children's Bureau of the Federal Security Agency show that since the all-out drive of the Drug Trust for drugging, vaccinating and serumizing the human system, the health of the American nation has sharply declined, especially among children. Children are now given "shots" for this and "shots" for that, when the only safeguard known to science is a pure bloodstream, which can be obtained only with clean air and wholesome food. Meaning by natural and inexpensive means. Just what the Drug Trust most objects to.

When the FDA, whose officials have to be acceptable to Rockefeller Center before they are appointed, has to put an independent operator out of business, it goes all out to execute those orders. But the orders do not come directly from Standard Oil or a drug house director. As Morris Bealle pointed out, the American Medical Association (AMA) is the front for the Drug Trust, and furnishes the quack doctors to testify that even when they know nothing of the product involved, it is their considered opinion that it has no therapeutic value.

Persecution

Wrote Bealle, "Financed by the taxpayers, these Drug Trust persecutions leave no stone unturned to destroy the victim. If he is a small operator, the resulting attorney's fees and court costs put him out of business. In one case, a Dr. Adolphus Hohensee of Scranton, Pa., who had stated that vitamins … were vital to good health, was taken to court for 'misbranding' his product. The American Medical Association furnished ten medicos who reversed all known medical theories by testifying that 'vitamins are not necessary to the human body.' Confronted with government bulletins to the contrary, the medicos [declared] that these standard publications were outdated!"

In addition to the FDA, Bealle listed the following agencies having to do with "health"—i.e., with the health of the Drug Trust to the detriment of the citizens—as being dependent on Rockefeller: U.S. Public Health Service, U.S. Veterans Administration, Federal Trade Commission, Surgeon General of the Air Force, Army Surgeon General's Office,Navy Bureau of Medicine & Surgery, National Health Research Institute, National Research Council, National Academy of Sciences.

The National Academy of Sciences in Washington is considered the all-wise body which investigates everything under the sun and gives to a palpitating public the last word in that science. To the important post at the head of this agency, the Drug Trust had one of their own appointed. He was none other than Alfred N. Richards, one of the directors and largest stockholders of Merck & Co., which was making huge profits from its drug traffic. When Bealle revealed this fact, Richards resigned forthwith, and the Rockefellers appointed in his place the President of their own Rockefeller Institution, Detlev W. Bronk.

America's Medico-Drug Cartel

The medico-drug cartel was summed up by J. W. Hodge, MD, of Niagara Falls, NY, in these words:

> The medical monopoly or medical trust, euphemistically called the American Medical Association, is not merely the meanest monopoly

ever organized, but the most arrogant, dangerous and despotic orga-nization which ever managed a free people in this or any other age. Any and all methods of healing the sick by means of safe, simple and natural remedies are sure to be assailed and denounced by the arro-gant leaders of the AMA doctors' trust as fakes, frauds and humbugs. Every practitioner of the healing art who does not ally himself with the medical trust is denounced as a "dangerous quack" and impos-tor by the predatory trust doctors. Every sanitarian who attempts to restore the sick to a state of health by natural means without resort to the knife or poisonous drugs, disease imparting serums, deadly toxins or vaccines, is at once pounced upon by these medical tyrants and fanatics, bitterly denounced, vilified and persecuted to the fullest extent.

The Lincoln Chiropractic College in Indianapolis requires 4,496 hours, the Palmer Institute Chiropractic in Davenport a minimum of 4,000 60-minute classroom hours, the University of Natural Healing Arts in Denver five years of 1,000 hours each to qualify for a degree. The National College of Naprapathy in Chicago requires 4,326 class-room hours for graduation. Yet the medico-drug cartel spreads the propaganda that the practitioners of these three "heretic" sciences are poorly trained or not trained at all—the real reason being that they cure their patients without the use of drugs.

In 1958, one of those "ill-trained" doctors, Nicholas P. Grimaldi, who had just graduated from the Lincoln Chiropractic College, took the basic science examination of the Connecticut State Board along with 63 medics and osteopaths. He made the highest mark (91.6) ever made by a doctor taking the Connecticut State Board examination.

Colonization

Rockefeller's various "educational" activities had proved so profitable in the u.s. that in 1927 the International Educational Board was launched, as Junior's own, personal charity, and endowed with $21,000,000 for a starter, to be lavished on foreign universities and politicos, with all the usual strings attached. This Board undertook to export the "new"

Rockefeller image as a benefactor of mankind, as well as his business practices. Nobody informed the beneficiaries that every penny the Rockefellers seemed to be throwing out the window would come back, bearing substantial interest, through the front door.

Rockefeller had always had a particular interest in China, where Standard Oil was almost the sole supplier of kerosene and oil "for the lamps of China". So he put up money to establish the China Medical Board and to build the Peking Union Medical College, playing the role of the Great White Father who has come to dispense knowledge on his lowly children.

The Rockefeller Foundation invested up to $45,000,000 into "westernizing" (read corrupting) Chinese medicine. Medical colleges were instructed that if they wished to benefit from the Rockefeller largesse they had better convince 500 million Chinese to throw into the ashcan the safe and useful but inexpensive herbal remedies of their barefoot doctors, which had withstood the test of centuries, in favor of the expensive carcinogenic and teratogenic "miracle" drugs "Made in USA," which had to be replaced constantly with new ones, when the fatal side-effects could no longer be concealed; and if they couldn't "demonstrate" through large-scale animal experiments the effectiveness of their ancient acupuncture, this could not be recognized as having any "scientific value". Its millenarian effectiveness proven on human beings was of no concern to the Western wizards. But when the communists came to power in China and it was no longer possible to trade, the Rockefellers suddenly lost interest in the health of the Chinese people and shifted their attention increasingly to Japan, India and Latin America.

The Image

No candid study of his career can lead to other conclusion than that he is victim of perhaps the ugliest of all passions, that for money, money as an end. It is not a pleasant picture... this moneymaniac secretly, patiently, eternally plotting how he may add to his wealth... He has turned commerce to war, and honey-combed it with cruel and corrupt practices... And he calls his great organization a benefaction,

and points to his churchgoing and charities as proof of his righteous-
ness. This is supreme wrong-doing cloaked by religion. There is but
one name for it—hypocrisy.

This was the description Ida Tarbell made of John D. Rockefeller in
her "History of the Standard Oil Company", serialized in 1905 in the
widely circulated *McClure's Magazine*. And that was several years before the Ludlow massacre, so JDR was as yet far from having reached
the apex of his disrepute. But after World War II it would have been
hard to read, in America or abroad, a single criticism of JDR, nor of
Junior, who had followed in his father's footsteps, nor of Junior's four
sons who all endevoured to emulate their illustrious forbears. Today's
various encyclopedias extant in public libraries of the Western world
have nothing but praise for the Family. How was this achieved?

Ironically, the two apparently most *negative* events in the career of
JDR brought about a huge *positive* change in his favor, to a degree that
he himself could not foresee. In the year when, according to the current *Encyclopaedia Britannica* (long become a Rockefeller property
and transferred from Oxford to Chicago), Rockefeller had "retired
from active business," namely in 1911, he had been convicted by a
U.S. court of illegal practices and ordered to dissolve the Standard
Oil Trust, which comprised 40 corporations. This imposed dissolution was to provide his Empire with added might, to a degree that
was unprecedented in the history of modem business. Until then,
the Trust had existed for all to see—an exposed target. After that, it
went underground, and thereby its power was cloaked in security,
and could keep expanding unseen and therefore unopposed. The
second apparently negative experience was a certain 1914 event that
persuaded JDR, until then utterly contemptuous of public opinion, to
gloss over his own image.

The Ludlow Massacre

The United Mine Workers had asked for higher wages and better
living conditions for the miners of the Colorado Fuel and Iron Company, one of the many Rockefeller-owned companies. The miners—

mostly immigrants from Europe's poorest countries—lived in shacks provided by the company at exorbitant rent. Their low wages ($1.68 a day) were paid in script redeemable only at company stores charging high prices. The churches they attended were the pastorates of company-hired ministers. Their children were taught in company-controlled schools.

The company maintained a force of detectives, mine guards, and spies whose job it was to keep the camp quarantined from the danger of unionization. When the miners struck, JDR, Jr., then officially in command of the company, and his father's hatchet man, the Baptist Reverend Frederick T. Gates, who was a director of the Rockefeller Foundation, refused even to negotiate. They evicted the strikers from the company-owned shacks, hired a thousand strikebreakers from the Baldwin-Felts detective agency, and persuaded Governor Ammons to call out the National Guard to help break the strike.

Open warfare resulted. Guardsmen, miners, their women and children, who since their eviction were camping in tents, were ruthlessly killed, until the frightened governor wired President Wilson for federal troops, who eventually crushed the strike. The *New York Times*, which then already could never be accused of being unfriendly to the Rockefeller interests, reported on April 21, 1914:

> A 14-hour battle between striking coal miners and members of the Colorado National Guard in the Ludlow district today culminated in the killing of Louis Tikas, leader of the Greek strikers, and the destruction of the Ludlow tent colony by fire.

And the following day:

> Forty-five dead (32 of them women and children), a score missing and more than a score wounded is the known result of the 14-hour battle which raged between state troops and coal miners in the Ludlow district, on the property of the Colorado Fuel and Iron Company, the Rockefeller holding. The Ludlow is a mass of charred debris, and buried beneath it is a story of horror unparalleled in the history of

industrial warfare. In the holes that had been dug for their protection against rifle fire, the women and children died like trapped rats as the flames swept over them. One pit uncovered this afternoon disclosed the bodies of ten children and two women.

Thorough Facelift

The worldwide revulsion that followed was such that JDR decided to hire the most talented press agent in the country, Ivy Lee, who got the tough assignment of whitewashing the tycoon's bloodied image. When Lee learned that the newly organized Rockefeller Foundation had $100 million lying around for promotional purposes without knowing what to do with it, he came with a plan to donate large sums, none less than a million, to well-known colleges, hospitals, churches and benevolent organizations. The plan was accepted. So were the millions. And they made headlines all over the world, for in the days of the gold standard and the five cent cigar there was a maxim in every newspaper office that a million dollars was always news.

That was the beginning of the cleverly worded medical reports on new "miracle" drugs and "just-around-the-corner breakthroughs" planted in the leading news offices and press associations that continue to this day, and the flighty public soon forgot, or forgave, the massacre of foreign immigrants for the dazzling display of generosity and philanthropy financed by the ballooning Rockefeller fortune and going out, with thunderous press fanfare, to various "worthy" institutions.

The Purchase of Public Opinion

In the following years, not only newsmen, but whole newspapers were bought, financed or founded with Rockefeller money. So, *Time* magazine, which Henry Luce started in 1923, had been taken over by J. P. Morgan when the magazine got into financial difficulties. When Morgan died and his financial empire crumbled, the House of Rockefeller wasted no time in taking over this lush editorial plum also, together with its sisters *Fortune* and *Life*, and built for them an expensive

14-story home of their own in Rockefeller Center—the Time & Life Building. Rockefeller was also co-owner of *Time*'s "rival" magazine, *Newsweek*, which had been established in the early days of the New Deal with money put up by Rockefeller, Vincent Astor, the Harriman family and other members and allies of the House.

The Intellectuals, a Bargain

For all his innate cynicism, JDR must have been himself surprised to discover how easily the so-called intellectuals could be bought. Indeed, they turned out to be among his best investments. By founding and lavishly endowing his Education Boards at home and abroad, Rockefeller won control not only of the governments and politicos but also of the intellectual and scientific community, starting with the Medical Power—the organization that forms those priests of the New Religion that are the modern medicine men. No Pulitzer or Nobel or any similar prize endowed with money and prestige has ever been awarded to a declared foe of the Rockefeller system.

Henry Luce, officially founder and editor of *Time* magazine, but constantly dependent on House advertising, also distinguished himself in his adulation of his sponsors. jdr's son had been responsible for the Ludlow massacre, and an obedient partner in his father's most unsavory actions. Nonetheless, in 1956, Henry Luce put Junior on the cover of *Time*, and the feature story, soberly titled "The Good Man," included hyperboles like this: "It is because John D. Rockefeller Junior's is a life of constructive social giving that he ranks as an authentic American hero, just as certainly as any general who ever won a victory for an American army or any statesman who triumphed in behalf of u.s. Diplomacy."

Clearly, *Time*'s editorial board wasn't given the choice to change its tune even after the passing of Junior and Henry Luce, since it remained just as dependent on House of Rockefeller advertising. When in 1979 one of Junior's sons, Nelson A. Rockefeller died—who had been one of the loudest hawks in the Vietnam and other American wars, and was personally responsible for the massacre of prisoners and hostages at Attica prison—*Time* said of him in it obituary, without laughing: "He was driven by a mission to serve, improve and up-lift his country." Perhaps it was all this that professor Peter Singer had in mind when telling the judges in Italy that the Rockefeller Foundation was a humanitarian enterprise bent on doing good works. One of their best works seems to be sponsoring professor Peter Singer, the world's greatest animal friend and protector who claims that vivisection is indispensable for medical progress and for more than 20 years refuses to mention that legions of medical doctors are of the opposite view.

Millions of Dollars Free Publicity

Another interesting revelation in the article of *Time* was that many years ago already Singer "was pleasantly surprised when *Britannica* approached him to distill in about 30,000 words the discipline that is, at its heart, the systematic study of what we ought to do."

So now we touch the subject of sponsorization and patronage. They don't always mean immediate cash but, more important, longterm profits. Many decades ago the *Encyclopaedia Britannica* moved from Oxford to Chicago, because Rockefeller had bought it to add much needed luster to the University of Chicago and its medical school, the first one he had founded.

Peter Singer, "the world's greatest animal defender" who keeps a door permanently open to vivisection and the lucrative medical swindle, gets millions of dollars free publicity thanks to the world-wide engagement of the Rockefeller Foundation and the media-makers who are in no position to oppose it.

From the article in *Time* we also learned that Singer's mother had been a medical doctor in the old country, which could mean that little Peter started assimilating all the Rockefeller superstition on vivisection with his mother's milk.

Published in issue 3 of The Dot Connector Magazine
(May-June 2009).

What Really Happened in Pont Saint Esprit

CIA's secret chemical warfare experiment
on unwitting inhabitants of a French village

By H. P. Albarelli, Jr.

On 13 February 2010, French TV channel France-3 broadcast the TV film Le Pain du diable *(The Devil's Bread; director Bertrand Arthuys, story by Olivier Dutaillis), which meticulously reconstructed the sinister incident happened in 1951 in the village of Pont Saint Esprit in southern France. It described the strange mass insanity that seized the village, as well as the interest of certain officials to cover up what really happened. A month later, on 13 March 2010, another French TV channel, France-2, has mentioned H. P. Albarelli Jr's new book,* A Terrible Mistake, *in the evening news, and even talked to the author on the phone... All this only to declare "pas convaincants" (non-convincing) his arguments that the inhabitants of Pont Saint Esprit were used as guinea pigs in a CIA-conducted mind control experiment which involved the aerosol spraying of LSD. Over sixty years after, the outbreak of madness in Pont Saint Esprit, which affected nearly five hundred people and caused 7 deaths, remains a "mystery" for the mainstream media...*

For decades now, the seemingly unrelated mysteries of Dr. Frank Olson's strange and alleged "suicide" in New York City in 1953 and the bizarre hallucinogenic outbreak of madness in a small French village in 1951 have independently provoked and perplexed serious investigators. As related in countless accounts on the internet and in televised news features, Olson's death has long been suspected to be a government-sponsored murder, but no plausible murderers or motives have ever been positively identified.

The outbreak of madness in the village of Pont St. Esprit in southern France has baffled scientists for decades, with many discounting strong suspicions of some sort of covert LSD attack simply because the means and motives were not believed to exist.

In 1995, I began to seriously investigate the death of Dr. Frank Olson, an American bacteriologist at the U.S. Army's top-secret biological warfare center at Fort Detrick, Maryland. Little did I suspect that my discovery that Olson was murdered would collide head on with the horrible events at Pont St. Esprit in August 1951.

My 900-page book, *A Terrible Mistake: The Murder of Frank Olson and the CIA's Secret Cold War Experiments*,[146] explains in painstaking detail how the two events collided. Recent reports that "a major diplomatic and political scandal is erupting that could have significant import for French-American relations" over my book's explanation about and documentation of the Pont St. Esprit outbreak causes me to provide an explanation here for those that are curious about the two events.

The strange outbreak of insanity in Pont St. Esprit affected nearly five hundred people, causing the deaths of at least five, and the suicides of two. For over sixty years, the incident has been tentatively attributed either to ergot poisoning, meaning villagers consumed bread infected with a psychedelic mold, or to mercury poisoning. The vast majority of credible scientists that examined the outbreak until recently have stated that the cause remains a mystery. A French newspaper at the time of the bizarre incident wrote,

> It is neither Shakespeare nor Edgar Poe. It is, alas, the sad reality all around Pont-St-Esprit and its environs, where terrifying scenes of hallucinations are taking place. They are scenes straight out of the Middle Ages, scenes of horror and pathos, full of sinister shadows.

---

146. H. P. Albarelli, Jr., *A Terrible Mistake: The Murder Of Frank Olson And The CIA's Secret Cold War Experiments*. TrineDay, January 2010. 960 pages.

A brief article in *Time* magazine, then a major U.S. news journal with extremely close ties to the CIA, stated,

> Among the stricken, delirium rose: patients thrashed wildly on their beds, screaming that red flowers were blossoming from their bodies.

Other newspapers that converged on the scene described people throwing themselves from rooftops, women and men throwing their cloths off and running the streets naked, and children complaining that their stomachs were infested with coils of snakes.

Shortly after the incident, in September 1951, scientists writing in the highly respected *British Medical Journal* declared that "the outbreak of poisoning" was produced by ergot mold. This explanation, however, was based almost solely upon the findings of biochemists dispatched to the scene from the nearby Sandoz Chemical Company in Basle, Switzerland. Included in the contingent from Sandoz was Dr. Albert Hofmann, the man who had first synthesized LSD on November 16, 1938. At the time of the Sandoz group's visit to Pont St. Esprit only a handful of scientists worldwide, estimated to be no more than eight-to-ten, knew of the existence of the man-made drug LSD. Of perhaps equal, if not greater, importance was that virtually nobody in France in 1951, apart from a select few officials at Sandoz Chemical, was aware that the company was secretly working closely with the CIA. Sandoz was both supplying the CIA with ample amounts of the drug, and consulting with the agency on possible defensive and offensive uses for LSD, including secret experimentation in the United States and Europe.

To grossly summarize the long story told in my book, the outbreak at Pont St. Esprit had actually been produced by a top-secret, joint Army-CIA experiment conducted as part of the Project MKNAOMI, an adjunct project to the CIA's ultra-secret Projects ARTICHOKE and MKULTRA. Indeed, the very unit that Dr. Frank Olson directed, the Special Operations Division at Fort Detrick, oversaw the experiment in France.

Suffice it to say I found the entire solution to the Pont St. Esprit mystery remarkably sensible and coherent, but also quite shocking, and I do not shock easily.

With further investigation the story became even more remarkable in its subtle features and obvious nature. Even today, a u.s. Department of Justice website on the dangers of LSD states that, in the early 1950s,

> ... the Sandoz Chemical Company went as far as promoting LSD as a potential secret chemical warfare weapon to the u.s. Government. Their main selling point in this was that a small amount in a main water supply or sprayed in the air could disorient and turn psychotic an entire company of soldiers leaving them harmless and unable to fight.

Not to mention, of course, an entire small town or city. Indeed, as I dug further into the overall story, I discovered once secret FBI documents that reveal that Fort Detrick's Special Operations Division had, one year prior to the Pont St. Esprit experiment, targeted *New York City's subway system* for a similar experiment. Reads an August 1950 FBI memorandum,

> The BW [biological warfare] experiments to be conducted by representatives of the Department of the Army in the New York Subway System in September 1950 have been indefinitely postponed.

When I discussed the FBI memoranda with former Fort Detrick biochemists, they confidentially informed me that the New York City experiments "were delayed until after the experiment was conducted in France."

Said one former Special Operations Division scientist:

> The overall results of the experiment in southern France were good, but there was also an adverse effect, or what would now be called a "black swan" reaction. That several people died was unexpected, completely unexpected. It wasn't supposed to turn out that way, so it was back to the drawing boards.

The same scientists confirmed that, following the Pont St. Esprit experiment, Fort Detrick's Special Operations Division returned to New York City in 1956 to conduct experiments under Operations Big City and Mad Hatter. These were covert projects that involved the aerosol spraying of chemicals through the exhaust pipe of an automobile that was driven by CIA and Army scientists around New York City. Prior to this, in 1952 and 1953, smaller experiments were conducted within New York subway cars by George Hunter White, a Federal Bureau of Narcotics agent, who secretly worked as a contractor for the CIA. On at least two occasions, White detonated specially devised aerosol devices filled with LSD. The CIA destroyed White's written reports covering these experiments in 1973.

Stepping backward for a moment to the time before I discovered the true cause of the southern France outbreak, perhaps the very first solid clue I had that something was amiss about the incident was a CIA confidential informer's report I had been given in 1999. That report, dated December 1953, concerned a meeting the unidentified informer had with an official of the Sandoz Chemical Company in New York City. The informer wrote that after "having several drinks" the Sandoz official blurted out, "The Pont Saint Esprit 'secret' was that it was not the bread at all." Continued the Sandoz official, "For weeks the French tied up our laboratories with analyses of bread. It was not the grain ergot, it was a diethylamide-like compound." By this, of course, the official meant a man-made drug had provoked the Pont St. Esprit outbreak.

The CIA informer then asked, according to his report, "If the material wasn't in the bread, then how did it get into the people?"

To this, the official responded, "An experiment." Now concerned, the informer asked, "An experiment?" To which the Sandoz official coyly responded, "Maybe by the French government," knowing that most likely the American informer well knew the identities of the actual perpetrators of the experiment. It was all an act of high political drama and subterfuge that concluded with the Sandoz official saying, "One small reason I'm here in the U.S. is to dispose of our LSD. If war breaks out, our LSD will disappear."

My next major clue in the chain of assembled evidence was a copy of a letter I was given that had been written by a Federal Narcotics agent who was also working for the CIA in the 1950s. This was George Hunter White. The letter written in October 1954 specifically referenced the Pont St. Esprit experiment, referring to it as "that little French village's Stormy epidemic." In White's veiled parlance with the CIA, "Stormy" was code for LSD.

Lastly, in the chain of evidence was an undated White House document that appeared to be part of a larger file that had been sent to members of the Rockefeller Commission formed in 1975 by President Gerald Ford to investigate the CIA abuses. The document contained the names of two French nationals who had been secretly employed by the CIA, and made direct reference to the "Pont St. Esprit incident" linking a former CIA biological warfare expert and the chief of Fort Detrick's Special Operations Division. This document, along with one other, in my view, comprised the smoking gun.

In 2005, a reporter with the *Baltimore Sun* newspaper, Scott Shane, who now writes for the *New York Times*, wrote, "The [U.S.] Army has no records on MKNAOMI or on the [Fort Detrick] Special Operations Division." When Scott, and then this writer, asked the Army for records on both, the Army replied that it "could find none." In 1973, the CIA destroyed all of its records on MKNAOMI and its work with Fort Detrick's Special Operations Division. One of the stated reasons for this destruction, explained the CIA, was that "people would not understand or misconstrue the reasons for many of the projects the Agency carried out." When reporter Shane asked a former top ranking Special Operations Division officer to speak about the division's past projects, Andrew M. Cowan, Jr., said, "I just don't give interviews on that subject. It should still be classified—if nothing else, to keep information the division developed out of the hands of some nut."

Earlier in the article, I wrote that I found the Pont St. Esprit experiment initially shocking. In many ways, I still do. But perhaps not for all those reasons many readers would imagine. Firstly, I find it shocking, when I read internet reactions to it, as contained in my book, over the past month like, "So what, at least they didn't do it in a small town in America!" Or worse yet, "Why didn't they pick a town in Mexico—it's closer by?" I'm saddened to find that some Americans have become both numb and immune to the arrogant and horrible past actions of the CIA. Torture is now supported in the United States by a large segment of the population. Some well-thinking Americans say that they pray for a return "to the America where their government honored, respected, and observed human rights and the international laws and treaties" that protected prisoners of war, enemy combatants, and detainees, but the real truth of the matter is that any objective and serious examination of Cold War history in America produces numerous instances of the horrific abuse of foreign detainees and prisoners.

The CIA's Project ARTICHOKE, throughout the 1950s and 1960s, subjected multiple foreign prisoners and suspected double agents to barbaric treatment, including electroshock therapy, lobotomies, and drug-induced insulin shock. Countless numbers of Americans were yanked off the streets of New York and San Francisco for secret experiments only because they were members of minority groups, poor, transient, perceived criminals, or prostitutes. Many of these people were permanently damaged physically and mentally because of these experiments. Nearly 6,500 U.S. servicemen were unwittingly subjected to LSD in the 1950s and 1960s. Many of these men never fully recovered from these experiments. Many committed suicide as a result of the experiments. In 1953, one foreign national was imprisoned and tortured for over eight months in Panama by the CIA only because he was suspected of cooperating with French intelligence officials. Later, the CIA may well have murdered the same man because he confidently told a news reporter that he knew who had murdered President John F. Kennedy.

Peter Levenda's revue of the book *A Terrible Mistake*

I don't want to give away the story that Hank Albarelli has uncovered, or any of the juicy details or important discoveries that will change the way you look at this case. You need to read this book carefully, cover to cover, to understand the enormity of what transpired that autumn evening in midtown Manhattan. The number of interconnected links between people, places and events is astounding. Familiar names like Dick Cheney and Donald Rumsfeld turn up, as well as Warren Burger and Rudolph Giuliani, Howard Hughes and Robert Maheu; less familiar names like John Rousselot, an American congressman, and John Bircher, accused of being involved in the assassination plot against President Kennedy, also make an appearance.

A walk through Hank Albarelli's masterful presentation of the Frank Olson case is like a tour of American political and cultural life during the last sixty years or more... And, at the same time, it is a descent into a very particular hell. (Is there such a thing as *negative* nostalgia?) Here we read of CIA's interest in the occult, in Edgar Cayce, UFOs, parapsychology, and in the strange visions of the Book of Ezekiel... I am not making this up.

Here we read of so many other victims of the mind control programs that we are forced to accept that Frank Olson represents only the tip of a Satanic iceberg. Innocent people were falling like flies all over America in the 1950s, like the textile plant workers in New Hampshire who were infected with anthrax without their knowledge, because their mill was doing work on the side in chemical and biological weapons research. Or the detective in Houston, Texas, who committed "suicide" by shooting himself in the heart ... twice.

If anyone has any doubts that Congress should investigate cases of torture and human rights abuses allegedly carried out by members of the intelligence community during the Iraq conflict, one only needs to review the Frank Olson case.

Our failure to fully investigate this scientist's death in 1953 contributed to further and ongoing abuses throughout the 1950s and 1960s. The very people—Cheney and Rumsfeld—who defended CIA's actions in those cases, when news of the CIA and military programs were exposed in 1975, would be defending them again decades later in a different guise and a different arena.

In those days, it was MKULTRA, MKNAOMI, MKOFTEN, MKCHICK-WIT, and of course Operations BLUEBIRD and ARTICHOKE. These are legendary names today; the stuff of pulp fiction and celluloid fantasy. But real people were drugged in those programs without their knowledge or consent. Men. Women. Children. Prisoners. Psychopaths. Prostitutes. Foreigners. Many of them were never the same again. Some went insane. Some died as a result. *And no one was held accountable.*

We have had Abu Ghraib, extraordinary rendition, waterboarding. Our excuse today—as it was then—is "national security." Hank Albarelli very helpfully reminds us of what Bella Abzug—the New York Congresswoman in the funny hats that the right wing loved to hate—said during the 1975 investigation of the CIA's mind control programs. She said:

> You cannot be strong outside if you are weak inside. You have to defend your own principles in order to be able to fight for acceptance of your principles in other places in the world... The question of the protection of our liberties and our freedom is the basis upon which this country remains strong.

That was in 1975. Forty years ago. What Hank Albarelli reminds us in this invaluable record of a "terrible mistake" is that we have yet to learn from those terrible mistakes. Or, more likely, not enough of us really care.

Hank Albarelli cares. And his concern is our gain. Part mystery story, part history, thoroughly documented and completely compelling, *A Terrible Mistake* is required reading for anyone interested in the lengths we have gone to defend the nation against all enemies (foreign, domestic, and the purely imaginary) ... and, incredibly, against our own loyal and patriotic citizens.

Published in issue 9 of The Dot Connector Magazine
(May-June 2010).

The Shocking True History
of human medical experimentation in the U.S.

The United States claims to be the world leader in medicine. But there's a dark side to Western medicine that few want to acknowledge: the horrifying medical experiments performed on impoverished people and their children all in the name of scientific progress. Many of these medical experiments were conducted on people without their knowledge, and most were conducted as part of an effort to seek profits from newly approved drugs or medical technologies. Today, the medical experiments continue on the U.S. population. Nearly 50% of Americans are on at least one prescription drug, and nearly 20% of schoolchildren are on mind-altering amphetamines like Ritalin or antidepressants like Prozac. This mass medication of the entire nation is, in every way, a grand medical experiment taking place right now. To truly understand how this mass experimentation on modern Americans came into being, you have to take a close look at the horrifying history of conventional medicine's exploitation of people for cruel medical experiments. **WARNING:** What you are about to read is truly shocking. You have never been told this information by the American Medical Association, nor drug companies, nor the evening news. This is the dark secret of the U.S. system of medicine, and once you read the true accounts reported here, you may never trust drug companies again. This information is deeply disturbing. We publish it here not as a form of entertainment, but as a stern warning against what might happen to us and our children if we do not rein in the horrifying, inhumane actions of Big Pharma and modern-day psychiatry. Read at your own risk.

—Mike Adams, *The Health Ranger, NaturalNews.com.*

The True U.S. History
of Human Medical Experimentation

By Dani Veracity

Human experimentation—that is, subjecting live human beings to science experiments that are sometimes cruel, sometimes painful, sometimes deadly and always a risk—is a major part of u.s. history that you won't find in most history or science books. The United States is undoubtedly responsible for some of the most amazing scientific breakthroughs. These advancements, especially in the field of medicine, have changed the lives of billions of people around the world—sometimes for the better, as in the case of finding a cure for malaria and other epidemic diseases, and sometimes for the worse (consider modern "psychiatry" and the drugging of schoolchildren).

However, these breakthroughs come with a hefty price tag: the human beings used in the experiments that made these advancements possible. Over the last two centuries, some of these test subjects have been compensated for the damage done to their emotional and physical health, but most have not. Many have lost their lives because of the experiments they often unwillingly and sometimes even unwittingly participated in, and they of course can never be compensated for losing their most precious possession of all: their health.

As you read through these science experiments, you'll learn the stories of newborns injected with radioactive substances, mentally ill people placed in giant refrigerators, military personnel exposed to chemical weapons by the very government they served, and mentally challenged children being purposely infected with hepatitis. These stories are facts, not fiction: each account, no matter how horrifying, is backed up with a reputable source.

These stories must be heard, because human experimentation is still going on today. The reasons behind the experiments may be different, but the usual human guinea pigs are still the same—members of minority groups, the poor, and the disadvantaged. These are the lives that were put on the line in the name of "scientific" medicine.

- **1833.** Dr. William Beaumont, an army surgeon physician, pioneers gastric medicine with his study of a patient with a permanently open gunshot wound to the abdomen and writes a human medical experimentation code that asserts the importance of experimental treatments, but also lists requirements stipulating that human subjects must give voluntary, informed consent and be able to end the experiment when they want. Beaumont's Code lists verbal, rather than just written, consent as permissible.

- **1845–1849.** J. Marion Sims, later hailed as the "father of gynecology," performs medical experiments on enslaved African women without anesthesia. These women would usually die of infection soon after surgery. Based on his belief that the movement of newborns' skull bones during protracted births causes trismus, he also uses a shoemaker's awl, a pointed tool shoemakers use to make holes in leather, to practice moving the skull bones of babies born to enslaved mothers.

- **1895.** New York pediatrician Henry Heiman infects a 4-year-old boy, whom he calls "an idiot with chronic epilepsy," with gonorrhea as part of a medical experiment.

- **1896.** Dr. Arthur Wentworth turns 29 children at Boston's Children's Hospital into human guinea pigs when he performs spinal taps on them, just to test whether the procedure is harmful.

- **1900.** U.S. Army doctors working in the Philippines infect five Filipino prisoners with plague and withhold proper nutrition to create beriberi in 29 prisoners. Four test subjects die.

- Under commission from the U.S. surgeon general, Dr. Walter Reed goes to Cuba and uses 22 Spanish immigrant workers to prove that yellow fever is contracted through mosquito bites. Doing so, he introduces the practice of using healthy test subjects, and also the concept of a written contract to confirm informed consent of these subjects. While doing this study, Dr. Reed clearly tells the subjects that, though he will do everything he can to help them, they may die as a result of the experiment. He pays them $100 in gold for their participation, plus $100 extra if they contract yellow fever.

- **1906.** Harvard professor Dr. Richard Strong infects prisoners in

175

the Philippines with cholera to study the disease; 13 of them die. He compensates survivors with cigars and cigarettes. (During the Nuremberg Trials, Nazi doctors cited this study to justify their own medical experiments.)

- **1911.** Dr. Hideyo Noguchi of the Rockefeller Institute for Medical Research publishes data on injecting an inactive syphilis preparation into the skin of 146 hospital patients and normal children in an attempt to develop a skin test for syphilis. Later, in 1913, several of these children's parents sue Dr. Noguchi for allegedly infecting their children with syphilis.

- **1913.** Medical experimenters "test" 15 children at the children's home St. Vincent's House in Philadelphia with tuberculin, resulting in permanent blindness in some of the children. Though the Pennsylvania House of Representatives records the incident, the researchers are not punished for the experiments.

- **1915.** Dr. Joseph Goldberger, under order of the u.s. Public Health Office, produces pellagra, a debilitating disease that affects the central nervous system, in 12 Mississippi inmates to try to find a cure for the disease. One test subject later says that he had been through "a thousand hells." In 1935, after millions die from the disease, the director of the Public Health Office would admit that officials had known that it was caused by a niacin deficiency for some time, but did nothing about it because it mostly affected poor African-Americans. (During the Nuremberg Trials, Nazi doctors used this study to try to justify their medical experiments on concentration camp inmates.)

- **1918.** In response to the Germans' use of chemical weapons during World War I, President Wilson creates the Chemical Warfare Service (cws) as a branch of the u.s. Army. Twenty-four years later, in 1942, the cws would begin performing mustard gas and lewisite experiments on over 4,000 members of the armed forces.

- **1919–1922.** Researchers perform testicular transplant experiments on inmates at San Quentin State Prison in California, inserting the testicles of recently executed inmates and goats into the abdomens and scrotums of living prisoners.

- **1931.** Cornelius Rhoads, a pathologist from the Rockefeller Institute for Medical Research, purposely infects human test subjects in Puerto Rico with cancer cells; 13 of them die. Though a Puerto Rican doctor later discovers that Rhoads purposely covered up some of details of his experiment and Rhoads himself gives a written testimony stating he believes that all Puerto Ricans should be killed, he later goes on to establish the u.s. Army Biological Warfare facilities in Maryland, Utah, and Panama, and is named to the u.s. Atomic Energy Commission, where he begins a series of radiation exposure experiments on American soldiers and civilian hospital patients.
- **1931–1933.** Mental patients at Elgin State Hospital in Illinois are injected with radium-266 as an experimental therapy for mental illness.
- **1932–1972.** The u.s. Public Health Service in Tuskegee, Alabama, diagnoses 400 poor, black sharecroppers with syphilis but never tells them of their illness nor treats them. Instead researchers use the men as human guinea pigs to follow the symptoms and progression of the disease. They all eventually die from syphilis and their families are never told that they could have been treated.
- **1937.** Scientists at Cornell University Medical School publish an angina drug study that uses both placebo and blind assessment techniques on human test subjects. They discover that the subjects given the placebo experienced more of an improvement in symptoms than those who were given the actual drug. This is the first account of the placebo effect published in the United States.
- **1939.** In order to test his theory on the roots of stuttering, prominent speech pathologist Dr. Wendell Johnson performs his famous "Monster Experiment" on 22 children at the Iowa Soldiers' Orphans' Home in Davenport. Dr. Johnson and his graduate students put the children under intense psychological pressure, causing them to switch from speaking normally to stuttering heavily. At the time, some of the students reportedly warn Dr. Johnson that, "in the aftermath of World War II, observers might draw comparisons to Nazi experiments on human subjects, which could destroy his career."

- **1941.** Dr. William C. Black infects a 12-month-old baby with herpes as part of a medical experiment.

o An article in a 1941 issue of *Archives of Pediatrics* describes medical studies of the severe gum disease Vincent's angina, in which doctors transmit the disease from sick children to healthy children with oral swabs.

o Drs. Francis and Salk and other researchers at the University of Michigan spray large amounts of wild influenza virus directly into the nasal passages of "volunteers" from mental institutions in Michigan. The test subjects develop influenza within a very short period of time.

o Researchers give 800 poverty-stricken pregnant women at a Vanderbilt University prenatal clinic "cocktails" including radioactive iron in order to determine the iron requirements of pregnant women.

- **1942.** The United States creates Fort Detrick, a 92-acre facility, employing nearly 500 scientists working to create biological weapons and develop defensive measures against them. Fort Detrick's main objectives include investigating whether diseases are transmitted by inhalation, digestion or through skin absorption. These biological warfare experiments heavily relied on the use of human subjects.

o U.S. Army and Navy doctors infect 400 prison inmates in Chicago with malaria to study the disease and hopefully develop a treatment for it. The prisoners are told that they are helping the war effort, but not that they are going to be infected with malaria. During Nuremberg Trials, Nazi doctors later cite this American study to defend their own medical experiments in concentration camps like Auschwitz.

o The Chemical Warfare Service begins mustard gas and lewisite experiments on 4,000 members of the U.S. military. Some test subjects don't realize they are volunteering for chemical exposure experiments, like 17-year-old Nathan Schnurman, who in 1944 thinks he is only volunteering to test "U.S. Navy summer clothes."

o Merck Pharmaceuticals President George Merck is named director of the War Research Service (WRS), an agency designed to oversee the establishment of a biological warfare program.

- **1943.** In order to "study the effect of frigid temperature on mental disorders," researchers at University of Cincinnati Hospital keep 16 mentally disabled patients in refrigerated cabinets for 120 hours at 30°F (−1°C).

- **1944.** As part of the Manhattan Project that would eventually create the atomic bomb, researchers inject 4.7 micrograms of plutonium into soldiers at the Oak Ridge facility, 20 miles west of Knoxville, Tennessee.

○ Captain A. W. Frisch, an experienced microbiologist, begins experiments on four volunteers from the state prison at Dearborn, Michigan, inoculating prisoners with hepatitis-infected specimens obtained in North Africa. One prisoner dies, two others develop hepatitis but live, the fourth develops symptoms but does not actually develop the disease.

○ Laboratory workers at the University of Minnesota and University of Chicago inject human test subjects with phosphorus-32 to learn the metabolism of hemoglobin.

○ A captain in the medical corps addresses an April 1944 memo to Col. Stafford Warren, head of the Manhattan Project's Medical Section, expressing his concerns about atom bomb component fluoride's central nervous system effects and asking for animal research to be done to determine the extent of these effects. The following year, the Manhattan Project would begin human-based studies on fluoride's effects.

○ The Manhattan Project medical team, led by the now infamous University of Rochester radiologist Col. Stafford Warren, injects plutonium into patients at the University's teaching hospital, Strong Memorial.

- **1944–1946.** In order to quickly develop a cure for malaria—a disease hindering Allied success in World War II—University of Chicago Medical School professor Dr. Alf Alving infects psychotic patients at Illinois State Hospital with the disease through blood transfusions and then experiments malaria cures on them.

- **1945.** Continuing the Manhattan Project, researchers inject plutonium into three patients at the University of Chicago's Billings Hospital.
  - The U.S. State Department, Army intelligence and the CIA begin Operation Paperclip, offering Nazi scientists immunity and secret identities in exchange for work on top secret government projects on aerodynamics and chemical warfare medicine in the United States.
  - Researchers infect 800 prisoners in Atlanta with malaria to study the disease.
- **1945–1955.** In Newburgh, NY, researchers linked to the Manhattan Project begin the most extensive American study ever done on the health effects of fluoridating public drinking water.
- **1946.** Gen. Douglas MacArthur strikes a secret deal with Japanese physician Dr. Shiro Ishii to turn over 10,000 pages of information gathered from human experimentation in exchange for granting Ishii immunity from prosecution for the horrific experiments he performed on Chinese, Russian and American war prisoners, including performing vivisections on live human beings.
  - Male and female test subjects at Chicago's Argonne National Laboratories are given intravenous injections of arsenic-76 so that researchers can study how the human body absorbs, distributes and excretes arsenic.
  - Continuing the Newburgh study of 1945, the Manhattan Project commissions the University of Rochester to study fluoride's effects on animals and humans in a project codenamed "Program F." With the help of the New York State Health Department, Program F researchers secretly collect and analyze blood and tissue samples from Newburgh residents. The studies are sponsored by the Atomic Energy Commission and take place at the University of Rochester Medical Center's Strong Memorial Hospital.
  - Six male employees of a Chicago metallurgical laboratory are given water contaminated with plutonium-239 to drink so that researchers can learn how plutonium is absorbed into the digestive tract.
  - Researchers begin using patients in Virginia hospitals as test sub-

jects for human medical experiments, cleverly worded as "investigations" or "observations" in medical study reports.

• **1946–1947.** University of Rochester researchers inject four male and two female human test subjects with uranium-234 and uranium-235 in dosages ranging from 6.4 to 70.7 micrograms per one kilogram of body weight in order to study how much uranium they could tolerate before their kidneys become damaged.

• **1946–1953.** The U.S. Atomic Energy Commission sponsors studies in which researchers from Harvard Medical School, Massachusetts General Hospital and the Boston University School of Medicine feed mentally disabled students at Fernald State School Quaker Oats breakfast cereal spiked with radioactive tracers every morning so that nutritionists can study how preservatives move through the human body and if they block the absorption of vitamins and minerals. Later, MIT researchers conduct the same study at Wrentham State School.

• Human test subjects are given one to four injections of arsenic-76 at the University of Chicago Department of Medicine. Researchers take tissue biopsies from the subjects before and after the injections.

• **1947.** Col. E. E. Kirkpatrick of the U.S. Atomic Energy Commission (AEC) issues a top-secret document (707075) dated January 8. In it, he writes that "certain radioactive substances are being prepared for intravenous administration to human subjects as a part of the work of the contract."

○ A secret AEC document dated April 17 reads: "It is desired that no document be released which refers to experiments with humans that might have an adverse reaction on public opinion or result in legal suits," revealing that the U.S. government was aware of the health risks its nuclear tests posed to military personnel conducting the tests or nearby civilians.

○ The CIA begins studying LSD's potential as a weapon by using military and civilian test subjects for experiments without their consent or even knowledge. Eventually, these LSD studies will evolve into the MKULTRA program in 1953.

- **1947–1953.** The U.S. Navy begins Project Chatter to identify and test so-called "truth serums," such as those used by the Soviet Union to interrogate spies. Mescaline and the central nervous system depressant scopolamine are among the many drugs tested on human subjects.
- **1948.** Based on the secret studies performed on Newburgh, NY, residents beginning in 1945, Project F researchers publish a report in the August 1948 edition of the *Journal of the American Dental Association*, detailing fluoride's health dangers. The U.S. Atomic Energy Commission (AEC) quickly censors it for "national security" reasons.
- **1950–1953.** The U.S. Army releases chemical clouds over six American and Canadian cities. Residents in Winnipeg, Canada, where a highly toxic chemical called cadmium is dropped, subsequently experience high rates of respiratory illnesses.
- The CIA and later the Office of Scientific Intelligence begin Project BLUEBIRD (renamed Project ARTICHOKE in 1951) in order to find ways to "extract" information from CIA agents, control individuals "through special interrogation techniques," "enhance memory" and use "unconventional techniques, including hypnosis and drugs," for offensive measures.
- **1951.** The U.S. Navy's Project BLUEBIRD is renamed Project ARTICHOKE and begins human medical experiments that test the effectiveness of LSD, sodium pentothal and hypnosis for the interrogative purposes described in Project BLUEBIRD's objectives.
- The U.S. Army secretly contaminates the Norfolk Naval Supply Center in Virginia and Washington, D.C.'s, National Airport with a strain of bacteria chosen because African-Americans were believed to be more susceptible to it than Caucasians. The experiment causes food poisoning, respiratory problems and blood poisoning.
- In order to determine how susceptible an American city could be to biological attack, the U.S. Navy sprays a cloud of *Bacillus globigii* bacteria from ships over the San Francisco shoreline. According to monitoring devices situated throughout the city to test the extent of infection, the 8,000 residents of San Francisco inhale 5,000 or

more bacteria particles, many becoming sick with pneumonia-like symptoms.

○ Dr. Joseph Strokes of the University of Pennsylvania infects 200 female prisoners with viral hepatitis to study the disease.

○ Doctors at the Cleveland City Hospital study changes in cerebral blood flow by injecting test subjects with spinal anesthesia, inserting needles in their jugular veins and brachial arteries, tilting their heads down and, after massive blood loss causes paralysis and fainting, measuring their blood pressure. They often perform this experiment multiple times on the same subject.

○ Dr. D. Ewen Cameron, later of MKULTRA infamy due to his 1957 to 1964 experiments on Canadians, publishes an article in the *British Journal of Physical Medicine*, in which he describes experiments that entail forcing schizophrenic patients at Manitoba's Brandon Mental Hospital to lie naked under 15 to 200-watt red lamps for up to eight hours per day. His other experiments include placing mental patients in an electric cage that overheats their internal body temperatures to 103°F (39.4°C), and inducing comas by giving patients large injections of insulin.

● **1951–1952.** Researchers withhold insulin from diabetic patients for up to two days in order to observe the effects of diabetes. Some test subjects go into diabetic comas.

● **1951–1956.** Under contract with the Air Force's School of Aviation Medicine (SAM), the University of Texas MD Anderson Cancer Center in Houston begins studying the effects of radiation on cancer patients (many of them members of minority groups or indigents, according to sources) in order to determine both radiation's ability to treat cancer and the possible long-term radiation effects of pilots flying nuclear-powered planes. The study lasts until 1956, involving 263 cancer patients. Beginning in 1953, the subjects are required to sign a waiver form, but it still does not meet the informed consent guidelines established by the Wilson memo released that year. The TBI studies themselves would continue at four different institutions—Baylor University College of Medicine, Memorial Sloan-Kettering Institute for Cancer Research, the U.S.

Naval Hospital in Bethesda, and the University of Cincinnati College of Medicine—until 1971.

o American, Canadian and British military and intelligence officials gather a small group of eminent psychologists to a secret meeting at the Ritz-Carlton Hotel in Montreal about communist "thought control techniques." They proposed a top-secret research program on behavior modification, involving testing drugs, hypnosis, electroshock and lobotomies on humans.

• **1952.** Military scientists use the Dugway Proving Ground (located 87 miles southwest of Salt Lake City, Utah) in a series of experiments to determine how *Brucella suis* and *Brucella melitensis* spread in human populations. Today, over a half-century later, some experts claim that we are all infected with these agents as a result of these experiments.

o In a U.S. Department of Defense-sponsored experiment, Henry Blauer dies after he is injected with mescaline at Columbia University's New York State Psychiatric Institute.

o At the famous Sloan-Kettering Institute, Chester M. Southam injects live cancer cells into prisoners at the Ohio State Prison to study the progression of the disease. Half of the prisoners in this National Institutes of Healthsponsored (NIH) study are black, awakening racial suspicions stemming from Tuskegee, which was also an NIH-sponsored study.

• **1953.** CIA Director Allen Dulles authorizes the MKULTRA program to produce and test drugs and biological agents that the CIA could use for mind control and behavior modification. MKULTRA later becomes well known for its pioneering studies on LSD, which are often performed on prisoners or patrons of brothels set up and run by the CIA. The brothel experiments, known as "Operation Midnight Climax," feature two-way mirrors set up in the brothels so that CIA agents can observe LSD's effects on sexual behavior. Ironically, governmental figures sometimes slip LSD into each other's drinks as part of the program, resulting in the LSD psychosis-induced suicide of Dr. Frank Olson indirectly at the hands of MKULTRA's infamous key player Dr. Sidney Gottlieb. Of all the hundreds of human test subjects used during MKULTRA, only 14 are ever notified of the involvement and only one is ever compensated ($15,000). Most of the MKULTRA files are eventually destroyed in 1973.

o The u.s. Atomic Energy Commission (AEC) sponsors iodine studies at the University of Iowa. In the first study, researchers give pregnant women 100 to 200 microcuries of iodine-131 and then study the women's aborted embryos in order to learn at what stage and to what extent radioactive iodine crosses the placental barrier. In the second study, researchers give 12 male and 13 female newborns under 36 hours old and weighing between 5.5 and 8.5 pounds iodine-131 either orally or via intramuscular injection, later measuring the concentration of iodine in the newborns' thyroid glands.

o As part of an AEC study, researchers feed 28 healthy infants at the University of Nebraska College of Medicine iodine-131 through a gastric tube and then test concentration of iodine in the infants' thyroid glands 24 hours later.

o In an AEC-sponsored study at the University of Tennessee, researchers inject healthy two to three-day-old newborns with approximately 60 rads of iodine-131.

o Newborn Daniel Burton becomes blind when physicians at Brooklyn Doctors Hospital perform an experimental high oxygen treatment for retrolental fibroplasia, a retinal disorder affecting premature infants, on him and other premature babies. The physicians perform the experimental treatment despite earlier studies showing that high oxygen levels cause blindness. Testimony in *Burton v. Brooklyn Doctors Hospital* later reveals that researchers continued to give Burton and other infants excess oxygen even after their eyes had swelled to dangerous levels.

o The CIA begins Project MKDELTA to study the use of biochemicals "for harassment, discrediting and disabling purposes."

o A 1953 article in *Clinical Science* describes a medical experiment in which researchers purposely blister the abdomens of 41 children, ranging in age from 8 to 14, with cantharide in order to study how severely the substance irritates the skin.

o The AEC performs a series of field tests known as "Green Run," dropping radiodine-131 and xenon-133 over the Hanford, Washington, site—500,000 acres encompassing three small towns (Hanford, White Bluffs and Richland) along the Columbia River.

o In an AEC-sponsored study to learn whether radioactive iodine affects premature babies differently from full-term babies, researchers at Harper Hospital in Detroit give oral doses of iodine-131 to 65 premature and full-term infants weighing between 2.1 and 5.5 pounds.

• **1953–1970.** The CIA begins project MKNAOMI to "stockpile incapacitating and lethal materials, to develop gadgetry for the disseminations of these materials, and to test the effects of certain drugs on animals and humans." As part of MKNAOMI, the CIA and the Special Operations Division of the Army Biological Laboratory at Fort Detrick try to develop two suicide pill alternatives to the standard cyanide suicide pill given to CIA agents and U-2 pilots. CIA agents and U-2 pilots are meant to take these pills when they find themselves in situations in which they (and all the information they hold in their brains) are in enemy hands. They also develop a "microbioinoculator"—a device that agents can use to fire small darts coated with biological agents that can remain potent for weeks or even months. These darts can be fired through clothing and, most significantly, are undetectable during autopsy. Eventually, by the late 1960s, MKNAOMI enables the CIA to have a stockpile of biological toxins—infectious viruses, paralytic shellfish toxin, lethal botulism toxin, snake venom and the severe skin disease-producing agent *Mircosporum gypseum*. The development of all of this "gadgetry" requires human experimentation.

• **1953–1957.** Eleven patients at Massachusetts General Hospital in Boston are injected with uranium as part of the Manhattan Project.

• **1954.** The CIA begins Project QKHILLTOP to study Chinese Communist Party brainwashing techniques and use them to further the CIA's own interrogative methods. Most experts speculate that the Cornell University Medical School Human Ecology Studies Program conducted Project QKHILLTOP's early experiments.

• **1954–1975.** U.S. Air Force medical officers assigned to Fort Detrick's Chemical Corps Biological Laboratory begin Operation

Whitecoat—experiments involving exposing human test subjects to hepatitis A, plague, yellow fever, Venezuelan equine encephalitis, Rift Valley fever, rickettsia and intestinal microbes. These test subjects include 2,300 Seventh Day Adventist military personnel, who choose to become human guinea pigs rather than potentially kill others in combat.

- **1955.** In U.S. Army-sponsored experiments performed at Tulane University, mental patients are given LSD and other drugs and then have electrodes implanted in their brain to measure the levels.
- **1955–1957.** In order to learn how cold weather affects human physiology, researchers give a total of 200 doses of iodine-131, a radioactive tracer that concentrates almost immediately in the thyroid gland, to 85 healthy Eskimos and 17 Athapascan Indians living in Alaska. They study the tracer within the body by blood, thyroid tissue, urine and saliva samples from the test subjects. No one explains the test subjects what is being done to them.
- **1955–1965.** As a result of their work with the CIA's mind control experiments in Project QKHILLTOP, Cornell neurologists Harold Wolff and Lawrence Hinkle begin the Society for the Investigation of Human Ecology (later renamed the Human Ecology Fund) to study "man's relation to his social environment as perceived by him."
- **1956–1957.** U.S. Army covert biological weapons researchers release mosquitoes infected with yellow fever and dengue fever over Savannah, Georgia, and Avon Park, Florida, to test the insects' ability to carry disease. After each test, Army agents pose as public health officials to test victims for effects and take pictures of the unwitting test subjects. These experiments result in a high incidence of fevers, respiratory distress, stillbirths, encephalitis and typhoid among the two cities' residents, as well as several deaths.
- **1957.** The U.S. military conducts Operation Plumbbob at the Nevada Test Site, 65 miles northwest of Las Vegas. Operation Plumbbob consists of 29 nuclear detonations, eventually creating radiation expected to result in a total 32,000 cases of thyroid cancer among civilians in the area. Around 18,000 members of the U.S. military participate in Operation Plumbbob's Desert Rock VII and

VIII, which are designed to see how the average foot soldier physiologically and mentally responds to a nuclear battlefield.

○ In order to study how blood flows through children's brains, researchers at Children's Hospital in Philadelphia perform the following experiment on healthy children, ranging in age from three to eleven. They insert needles into each child's femoral artery (thigh) and jugular vein (neck), bringing the blood down from the brain. Then, they force each child to inhale a special gas through a facemask. In their subsequent *Journal of Clinical Investigation* article on this study, the researchers note that, in order to perform the experiment, they had to restrain some of the child test subjects by bandaging them to boards.

● **1957–1964.** As part of MKULTRA, the CIA pays McGill University Department of Psychiatry founder Dr. D. Ewen Cameron $69,000 to perform LSD studies and potentially lethal experiments on Canadians being treated for minor disorders like postpartum depression and anxiety at the Allan Memorial Institute, which houses the Psychiatry Department of the Royal Victoria Hospital in Montreal. The CIA encourages Dr. Cameron to fully explore his "psychic driving" concept of correcting madness through completely erasing one's memory and rewriting the psyche. These "driving" experiments involve putting human test subjects into drug-, electroshock- and sensory deprivation-induced vegetative states for up to three months, and then playing tape loops of noise or simple repetitive statements for weeks or months in order to "rewrite" the "erased" psyche. Dr. Cameron also gives human test subjects paralytic drugs and electroconvulsive therapy 30 to 40 times, as part of his experiments. Most of Dr. Cameron's test subjects suffer permanent damage as a result of his work.

● **1958.** Approximately 300 members of the U.S. Navy are exposed to radiation when the Navy destroyer *Mansfield* detonates 30 nuclear bombs off the coasts of Pacific Islands during Operation Hardtack.

○ The U.S. Atomic Energy Commission (AEC) drops radioactive materials over Point Hope, Alaska, home to the Inupiats, in a field test known under the codename "Project Chariot."

- **1961.** In response to the Nuremberg Trials, Yale psychologist Stanley Milgram begins his famous Obedience to Authority Study in order to answer his question: "Could it be that (Adolf) Eichmann and his million accomplices in the Holocaust were just following orders? Could we call them all accomplices?" Male test subjects, ranging in age from 20 to 40 and coming from all education backgrounds, are told to give "learners" electric shocks for every wrong answer the learners give in response to word pair questions. In reality, the learners are actors and are not receiving electric shocks, but what matters is that the test subjects do not know that. Astoundingly, they keep on following orders and continue to administer increasingly high levels of "shocks," even after the actor learners show obvious physical pain.

- **1962.** Researchers at the Laurel Children's Center in Maryland test experimental acne antibiotics on children and continue their tests even after half of the young test subjects develop severe liver damage because of the experimental medication. The U.S. Army's Deseret Test Center begins Project 112. This includes SHAD (Shipboard Hazard and Defense), which exposes U.S. Navy and Army personnel to live toxins and chemical poisons in order to determine naval ships' vulnerability to chemical and biological weapons. Military personnel are not test subjects; conducting the tests exposes them. Many of these participants complain of negative health effects at the time and, decades later, suffer from severe medical problems as a result of their exposure.

- The FDA begins requiring that a new pharmaceutical undergo three human clinical trials before it will approve it. From 1962 to 1980, pharmaceutical companies satisfy this requirement by running Phase I trials, which determine a drug's toxicity, on prison inmates, giving them small amounts of cash for compensation.

- **1963.** Chester M. Southam, who injected Ohio State Prison inmates with live cancer cells in 1952, performs the same procedure on 22 senile, African-American female patients at the Brooklyn Jewish Chronic Disease Hospital in order to watch their immunological response. Southam tells the patients that they are receiving "some cells," but leaves out the fact that they are cancer cells. He claims he doesn't obtain informed consent from the patients because he does not want to frighten them by telling them what he is doing, but he nevertheless temporarily loses his medical license because of it. Ironically, he eventually becomes president of the American Cancer Society.

o Researchers at the University of Washington directly irradiate the testes of 232 prison inmates in order to determine radiation's effects on testicular function. When these inmates later leave prison and have children, at least four have babies born with birth defects. The exact number is unknown, because researchers never follow up on the men to see the longterm effects of their experiment.

o In a National Institutes of Health-sponsored (NIH) study, a researcher transplants a chimpanzee's kidney into a human. The experiment fails.

o Researchers inject a genetic compound called radioactive thymidine into the testicles of more than 100 Oregon State Penitentiary inmates to learn whether sperm production is affected by exposure to steroid hormones.

o In a study published in *Pediatrics*, researchers at the University of California's Department of Pediatrics use 113 newborns ranging in age from one hour to three days old in a series of experiments used to study changes in blood pressure and blood flow. In one study, doctors insert a catheter through the newborns' umbilical arteries and into their aortas and then immerse the newborns' feet in ice water while recording aortic pressure. In another experiment, doctors strap 50 newborns to a circumcision board, tilt the table so that all the blood rushes to their heads and then measure their blood pressure.

• **1963–1966.** New York University researcher Saul Krugman promises parents with mentally disabled children definite enrollment into the Willowbrook State School in Staten Island, NY, a resident mental institution for mentally retarded children, in exchange for their signatures on a consent form for procedures presented as "vaccinations." In reality, the procedures involve deliberately infecting children with viral hepatitis by feeding them an extract made from the feces of infected patients, so that Krugman can study the course of viral hepatitis as well the effectiveness of a hepatitis vaccine.

- **1963–1971.** Leading endocrinologist Dr. Carl Heller gives 67 prison inmates at Oregon State Prison in Salem $5 per month and $25 per testicular tissue biopsy in compensation for allowing him to perform irradiation experiments on their testes. If they receive vasectomies at the end of the study, the prisoners are given an extra $100.

- **1964–1968.** The U.S. Army pays $386,486 (the largest sum ever paid for human experimentation) to University of Pennsylvania professors Albert Kligman and Herbert W. Copeland to run medical experiments on 320 inmates of Holmesburg Prison to determine the effectiveness of seven mind-altering drugs. The researchers' objective is to determine the minimum effective dose of each drug needed to disable 50 percent of any given population (MED-50). Though professors Kligman and Copeland claim that they are unaware of any long-term effects the mind-altering agents might have on prisoners, documents revealed later would prove otherwise.

- **1964–1967.** The Dow Chemical Company pays prof. Kligman $10,000 to learn how dioxin—a highly toxic, carcinogenic component of Agent Orange—and other herbicides affect human skin, because workers at the chemical plant have been developing an acne-like condition called *chloracne* and the company would like to know whether the chemicals they are handling are to blame. As part of the study, prof. Kligman applies roughly the amount of dioxin Dow employees are exposed to on the skin 60 prisoners, and is disappointed when the prisoners show no symptoms of *chloracne*. In 1980 and 1981, the human guinea pigs used in this study would begin suing prof. Kligman for complications including lupus and psychological damage.

- **1965.** As part of a test codenamed "Big Tom," the Department of Defense sprays Oahu, Hawaii's most heavily populated island, with *Bacillus globigii* in order to simulate an attack on an island complex. *Bacillus globigii* causes infections in people with weakened immune systems, but this was not known to scientists at the time.

- **1966.** The CIA continues a limited number of MKULTRA plans by beginning Project MKSEARCH to develop and test ways of using biological, chemical and radioactive materials in intelligence operations, and also to develop and test drugs that are able to produce predictable changes in human behavior and physiology.

- U.S. Army scientists drop light bulbs filled with *Bacillus subtilis* through ventilation gates and into the New York City subway system, exposing more than one million civilians to the bacteria.

- **1967.** Continuing on his Dow Chemical Company-sponsored dioxin study without the company's knowledge or consent, University of Pennsylvania prof. Albert Kligman increases the dosage of dioxin he applies to 10 prisoners' skin to 7,500 micrograms, 468 times the dosage Dow official Gerald K. Rowe had authorized him to administer. As a result, the prisoners experience acne lesions that develop into inflammatory pustules and papules.

- The CIA places a chemical in the drinking water supply of the FDA headquarters in Washington, D.C., to see whether it is possible to spike drinking water with LSD and other substances.

- In a study published in the *Journal of Clinical Investigation*, researchers inject pregnant women with radioactive cortisol to see if the radioactive material will cross the placentas and affect the fetuses.

- The U.S. Army pays prof. Kligman to apply skin-blistering chemicals to Holmesburg Prison inmates' faces and backs, so as to, in prof. Kligman's words, "learn how the skin protects itself against chronic assault from toxic chemicals, the so-called hardening process," information which would have both offensive and defensive applications for the U.S. military.

- The CIA and Edgewood Arsenal Research Laboratories begin an extensive program for developing drugs that can influence human behavior. This program includes Project OFTEN, which studies the toxicology, transmission and behavioral effects of drugs in animal and human subjects, and Project CHICKWIT, which gathers European and Asian drug development information.

- Prof. Kligman develops Retin-A as an acne cream (and eventually a wrinkle cream), turning him into a multimillionaire.

○ Researchers paralyze 64 prison inmates in California with a neuro-muscular compound called succinylcholine, which produces suppressed breathing that feels similar to drowning. When five prisoners refuse to participate in the medical experiment, the prison's special treatment board gives researchers permission to inject the prisoners with the drug against their will.

● **1968.** Planned Parenthood of San Antonio and South Central Texas and the Southwest Foundation for Research and Education begin an oral contraceptive study on 70 poverty-stricken Mexican-American women, giving only half the oral contraceptives they think they are receiving and the other half a placebo. When the results of this study are released a few years later, it stirs tremendous controversy among Mexican-Americans.

● **1969.** Experimental drugs are tested on mentally disabled children in Milledgeville, Georgia, without any institutional approval whatsoever.

● **1970.** A year after his request under HR 15090, Dr. Donald MacArthur receives funding to begin CIA-supervised mycoplasma research with Fort Detrick's Special Operations Division and hopefully create a synthetic immunosuppressive agent. Some experts believe that this research may have inadvertently created HIV, the virus that causes AIDS.

○ Under order from the National Institutes of Health (NIH), which also sponsored the Tuskegee Experiment, the free childcare program at Johns Hopkins University collects blood samples from 7,000 African-American youth, telling their parents that they are checking for anemia but actually checking for an extra Y chromosome (XYY), believed to be a biological predisposition to crime. The program director, Digamber Borganokar, does this experiment without Johns Hopkins University's permission.

● **1971.** Stanford University conducts the Stanford Prison Experiment on a group of college students in order to learn the psychology of prison life. Some students are given the role as prison guards, while the others are given the role of prisoners. After only six days, the proposed two-week study has to end because of its psychological effects on the participants. The "guards" had begun to act sadistic, while the "prisoners" started to show signs of depression and severe psychological stress.

- **1972.** In studies sponsored by the U.S. Air Force, Dr. Amedeo Marrazzi gives LSD to mental patients at the University of Missouri Institute of Psychiatry and the University of Minnesota Hospital to study "ego strength."

- **1978.** The CDC begins experimental hepatitis B vaccine trials in New York. Its ads for research subjects specifically ask for promiscuous homosexual men. Professor Wolf Szmuness of the Columbia University School of Public Health had made the vaccine's infective serum from the pooled blood serum of hepatitis-infected homosexuals and then developed it in chimpanzees, the only animal susceptible to hepatitis B, leading to the theory that HIV originated in chimpanzees before being transferred over to humans via this vaccine. A few months after 1,083 homosexual men receive the vaccine, New York physicians begin noticing cases of Kaposi's sarcoma, *Mycoplasma penetrans* and a new strain of herpes virus among New York's homosexual community—diseases not usually seen among young men, but that would later be known as common opportunistic diseases associated with AIDS.

- **1980.** A study reveals a high incidence of leukemia among the 18,000 military personnel who participated in 1957's Operation Plumbbob.

- According to blood samples tested years later for HIV, 20% of all New York homosexual men who participated in the 1978 hepatitis B vaccine experiment are HIV-positive by this point.

- Experimental hormone shots are given to hundreds of Haitian men confined to detention camps in Miami and Puerto Rico, causing the men to develop a condition known as gynecomastia, in which men develop full-sized breasts.

- The CDC continues its 1978 hepatitis B vaccine experiment in Los Angeles, San Francisco, Chicago, St. Louis and Denver, recruiting over 7,000 homosexual men in San Francisco alone.

- The first AIDS case appears in San Francisco.

- **1981.** A deep diving experiment at Duke University causes test subject Leonard Whitlock to suffer permanent brain damage.

o The CDC acknowledges the existence of AIDS and confirms 26 cases of the disease—all in previously healthy homosexuals living in New York, San Francisco and Los Angeles—again supporting the speculation that AIDS originated from the hepatitis B experiments from 1978 and 1980.

- **1981–1993.** The Seattle-based Genetic Systems Corporation begins an ongoing medical experiment called Protocol No. 126, in which patients at the Fred Hutchinson Cancer Research Center in Seattle are given bone marrow transplants that contain eight experimental proteins made by Genetic Systems, rather than standard bone marrow transplants. 19 human subjects die from complications directly related to the experimental treatment.

- **1982.** Thirty percent of the test subjects used in the CDC's hepatitis B vaccine experiment are HIV-positive by this point.

- **1984.** SFBC Phase I research clinic founded in Miami, Florida. By 2005, it would become the largest experimental drug testing center in North America with centers in Miami and Montreal, running Phase I to Phase IV clinical trials.

- **1985.** A former U.S. Army sergeant tries to sue the Army for using drugs on him without his consent or even his knowledge in *United States v. Stanley, 483 U.S. 669.* Justice Antonin Scalia writes the decision, clearing the U.S. military from any liability in past, present or future medical experiments without informed consent.

- **1987.** Philadelphia resident Doris Jackson discovers that researchers have removed her son's brain post mortem for medical study. She later learns that the state of Pennsylvania has a doctrine of "implied consent," meaning that unless a patient signs a document stating otherwise, consent for organ removal is automatically implied.

- **1988.** The U.S. Justice Department pays nine Canadian survivors of the CIA and Dr. Cameron's "psychic driving" experiments (1957–1964) $750,000 in out-of-court settlements, to avoid any further investigations into MKULTRA.

- **1988–2001.** The New York City Administration for Children's Services begins allowing foster care children living in about two dozen children's homes to be used in National Institutes of Health-sponsored (NIH) experimental AIDS drug trials. These children—totaling 465 by the program's end—experience serious side effects, including inability to walk, diarrhea, vomiting, swollen joints and cramps.
- **1990.** The United States sends 1.7 million members of the armed forces, 22 percent of whom are African-American, to the Persian Gulf for the Gulf War ("Desert Storm"). More than 400,000 of these soldiers are ordered to take an experimental nerve agent called pyridostigmine, which is later believed to be the cause of Gulf War Syndrome—symptoms ranging from skin disorders, neurological disorders, incontinence, uncontrollable drooling and vision problems—affecting Gulf War veterans.
- ○ The CDC and Kaiser Pharmaceuticals of Southern California inject 1,500 six-month-old black and Hispanic babies in Los Angeles with an "experimental" measles vaccine that had never been licensed for use in the U.S. Adding to the risk, children less than a year old may not have an adequate amount of myelin around their nerves, possibly resulting in impaired neural development because of the vaccine. The CDC later admits that parents were never informed that the vaccine being injected into their children was experimental.
- ○ The FDA allows the U.S. Department of Defense to waive the Nuremberg Code and use unapproved drugs and vaccines in Operation Desert Shield.
- **1991.** In the May 27 issue of the *Los Angeles Times*, former U.S. Navy radio operator Richard Jenkins writes that he suffers from leukemia, chronic fatigue and kidney and liver disease as a result of the radiation exposure he received in 1958's Operation Hardtack.
- ○ While participating in a UCLA study that withdraws schizophrenics off of their medication, Tony LaMadrid commits suicide.
- **1992.** Columbia University's New York State Psychiatric Institute and the Mount Sinai School of Medicine give 100 males—mostly African-American and Hispanic, all between the ages of 6 and 10 and all the younger brothers of juvenile delinquents—10 milli-

grams of fenfluramine (fen-fen) per kilogram of body weight in order to test the theory that low serotonin levels are linked to violent or aggressive behavior. Parents of the participants received $125 each, including a $25 Toys 'R' Us gift certificate.

- **1993.** Researchers at the West Haven VA in Connecticut give 27 schizophrenics—12 inpatients and 15 functioning volunteers—a chemical called MCPP that significantly increases their psychotic symptoms and, as researchers note, negatively affects the test subjects on a long-term basis.

- **1994.** In a double-blind experiment at New York VA Hospital, researchers take 23 schizophrenic inpatients off of their medications for a median of 30 days. They then give 17 of them 0.5 mg/kg amphetamine and six a placebo as a control, following up with PET scans at Brookhaven Laboratories. According to the researchers, the purpose of the experiment was "to specifically evaluate metabolic effects in subjects with varying degrees of amphetamine-induced psychotic exacerbation."

- Researchers at Bronx VA Medical Center recruit 28 schizophrenic veterans who are functioning in society and give them L-dopa in order to induce psychotic relapse.

- **1995.** A 19-year-old University of Rochester student named Nicole Wan dies from participating in an MIT-sponsored experiment that tests airborne pollutant chemicals on humans. The experiment pays $150 to human test subjects.

- In Dr. Daniel P. van Kammen's study, "Behavioral vs. Biochemical Prediction of Clinical Stability Following Haloperidol Withdrawal in Schizophrenia," researchers recruit 88 veterans who are stabilized by their medications enough to make them functional in society, and hospitalize them for 8 to 10 weeks. During this time, the researchers stop giving the veterans the medications that are enabling them to live in society, placing them back on a two to four-week regimen of the standard dose of Haldol. Then the veterans are "washed-out," given lumbar punctures and put under six-week observation to see who would relapse and suffer symptomatic schizophrenia once again; 50 percent do.

o President Clinton "apologizes" to the thousands of people who were victims of MKULTRA and other mind control programs.

● **1996.** Professor Adil E. Shamoo of the University of Maryland and the organization Citizens for Responsible Care and Research send a written testimony on the unethical use of veterans in medical research to the U.S. Senate's Committee on Governmental Affairs, stating: "This type of research is ongoing nationwide in medical centers and VA hospitals supported by tens of millions of dollars of taxpayers money. These experiments are high risk and are abusive, causing not only physical and psychic harm to the most vulnerable groups, but also degrading our society's system of basic human values. Probably tens of thousands of patients are being subjected to such experiments."

o The Department of Defense admits that Gulf War soldiers were exposed to chemical agents. However, 33 percent of all military personnel afflicted with Gulf War Syndrome never left the United States during the war, discrediting the popular mainstream belief that these symptoms are a result of exposure to Iraqi chemical weapons.

o In a federally funded experiment at West Haven VA in Connecticut, Yale University researchers give schizophrenic veterans amphetamine, even though central nervous system stimulants worsen psychotic symptoms in 40 percent of schizophrenics.

● **1997.** National Institutes of Mental Health (NIMH) researchers give schizophrenic veterans amphetamine, even though central nervous system stimulants worsen psychotic symptoms in 40 percent of schizophrenics.

o In an experiment sponsored by the U.S. government, researchers withhold medical treatment from HIV-positive African-American pregnant women, giving them a placebo rather than AIDS medication.

o Researchers give amphetamine to 13 schizophrenic patients in a repetition of the 1994 "amphetamine challenge" at New York VA Hospital. As a result, the patients experience psychosis, delusions and hallucinations.

- **1999.** Doctors at the University of Pennsylvania inject 18 year-old Jesse Gelsinger with an experimental gene therapy as part of an FDA-approved clinical trial. He dies 4 days later.
- During a clinical trial investigating the effectiveness of Propulsid for infant acid reflux, nine-month-old Gage Stevens dies at Children's Hospital in Pittsburgh.
- **2000.** The Department of Defense begins declassifying the records of Project 112, including SHAD, and locating and assisting the veterans who were exposed to live toxins and chemical agents as part of Project 112. Many of them have already died.
- The U.S. Air Force and rocket maker Lockheed Martin sponsor a Loma Linda University study that pays 100 Californians $1,000 to eat a dose of perchlorate—a toxic component of rocket fuel that causes cancer, damages the thyroid gland and hinders normal development in children and fetuses—every day for six months. The dose eaten by the test subjects is 83 times the safe dose of perchlorate set by the State of California, which has perchlorate in some of its drinking water. This Loma Linda study is the first large-scale study to use human subjects to test the harmful effects of a water pollutant.
- **2001.** Healthy 27-year-old Ellen Roche dies in a challenge study at Johns Hopkins University in Maryland.
- During a tobacco industry-financed Alzheimer's experiment at Case Western University in Cleveland, Elaine Holden-Able dies after she drinks a glass of orange juice containing a dissolved dietary supplement.
- Radiologist Scott Scheer of Pennsylvania dies from kidney failure, severe anemia, and possibly lupus—all caused by blood pressure drugs he was taking as part of a five-year clinical trial.

*Published in issue 8 of The Dot Connector Magazine
(March-April 2010).*

Secret Weather Wars

Jerry E. Smith (1950–2010)

"If man can modify the weather, he will obviously modify it for military purposes. It is no coincidence that the u.s. Army, Navy, Air Force and Signal Corps have been deeply involved in weather modification research and development. Weather is a weapon, and the general who has control over the weather is in control of an opponent less well armed… The idea of clobbering an enemy with a blizzard, or starving him with an artificial drought, still sounds like science fiction. But so did talk of atom bombs before 1945." So wrote author Daniel S. Halacy, Jr., in his book, *The Weather Changers*, published in 1968.

Modern scientific attempts to control the weather began with Bernard Vonnegut's discovery in 1946 that microscopic crystals of silver iodide (AgI) nucleate water vapor to form ice crystals. His breakthrough invention of a practical way of generating tiny AgI particles to serve as nuclei for ice crystals led to the modern practice of cloud seeding. More than fifty years later his method continues to be the most common. Control of the weather, at least to some degree, is today an established and expanding field of scientific and commercial endeavor across North America and around the world.

Uncle Sam's Disappearing Federal Budget Trick

Mankind has always had a keen interest in the weather. Throughout human history we have seen the effects of weather on crops, and the loss of life and property through the violence of storms. In ancient times people made sacrifice to the gods in a crude attempt at influencing the weather. In many parts of the world today people still conduct elaborate rituals for rain and fertility.

The modern interest in making rain for profit and/or the public good began, surprisingly enough, following the American Civil War. A large volume of literature on the subject was generated between 1890 and 1894 alone. Martha B. Caldwell in her article "Some Kansas Rain Makers," published in the *Kansas Historical Quarterly* in August of 1938, summed up much of this material. She wrote:

> These writers had various theories as to the methods of producing rain. A French author suggested using a kite to obtain electrical connections with the clouds. James P. Espy, a meteorologist from Pennsylvania, proposed the method of making rain by means of fires. This idea is prevalent on the Western Plains where the saying, "A very large prairie fire will cause rain," has almost become a proverb. The Indians on the plains of South America were accustomed to setting fire to the prairies when they wanted rain. A third method, patented by Louis Gathman in 1891, was based on the supposition that sudden chilling of the upper atmosphere by releasing compressed gases would cause rapid evaporation and thus produce rain. One of the oldest theories of producing artificial rain is known as the concussion theory, or that of generating moisture by great explosions. The idea originated from the supposition that heavy rains follow great battles. Gen. Daniel Ruggles of Fredericksburg, Va., obtained a patent on the concussion theory in 1880, and urged congress to appropriate funds for testing it.
>
> By 1890, the subject of artificial rain making had attained considerable dignity; two patents had been issued and through the efforts of Sen. C. B. Farwell, Congress had made appropriations, $2,000 first, and then $7,000, to carry on experiments. In 1892 an additional appropriation of $10,000 was made to continue the work. The carrying out of these experiments naturally fell to the Department of Agriculture, and the Secretary selected R. G. Dryenforth to conduct them. In 1891, Mr. Dryenforth with his assistants proceeded to the "Staked Plains of Texas" to begin work. Included in the equipment which he

took with him were sixty-eight explosive balloons, three large balloons for making ascensions, and material for making one hundred cloth-covered kites, besides the necessary explosives, etc. He used the explosives both on the ground and in the air. An observer stated that "it was a beautiful imitation of a battle." The balloons filled with gas were exploded high in the atmosphere. After a series of experiments carried on in different parts of Texas over a period of two years, his conclusions were to the effect that under favorable conditions precipitation may be caused by concussion, and that under unfavorable conditions "storm conditions may be generated and rain be induced, there being, however, a wasteful expenditure of both time and material in overcoming unfavorable conditions."

Twenty thousand dollars in 1890 would have the purchasing power of about a quarter million today. Over the next eighty years, Congress maintained an on again, off again interest in funding this research. One notable expenditure occurred in 1967, when the U.S. Senate passed the Magnusson Bill authorizing the Secretary of Commerce to accelerate programs of applied research, development and experimentation in weather and climate modification. That bill allocated $12 million, $30 million, and $40 million over the next three years, respectively. They projected expenditures of some $149 million annually by 1970.

It can be argued that, by the beginning of the 1970s, portions of the U.S. government and/or military viewed weather and climate modification research as having transitioned from the "basic research" stage to the "operational" stage. Experiments were occurring—or had occurred—in 22 countries, including Argentina, Australia, Canada, Iran, Israel, Kenya, Italy, France, South Africa, Congo, and the U.S.S.R. Airborne seeding programs were undertaken to combat drought in the Philippines, Okinawa, Africa, and Texas. Fog clearing had become a standard operation at airports, as had hailstorm abatement, which had been proven successful in several parts of the world. Forest fire control had been carried out in Alaska, and watershed seeding was widely practiced, while lake storm snow redistribution was under extensive investigation. By 1973, there were over 700 degreed scientists and engineers in the u.s., whose major occupation was environmental modification (EnMod).

And then it all changed. In 1978, the United States became a signatory to the United Nations Convention on the Prohibition of Military or Any Other Hostile Use of Environmental Modification Techniques (EnMod Convention, or EnMod for short). The EnMod Convention prohibits the use of techniques that would have widespread, long-lasting or severe effects through deliberate manipulation of natural processes and cause such phenomena as earthquakes, tidal waves and changes in climate and weather patterns.

Independent journalist Keith Harmon Snow wrote a massive report entitled "Out of the Blue: Black Programs, Space Drones & The Unveiling of u.s. Military Offensives in Weather as a Weapon." In it he tells us:

> In 1976, u.s. government officials outlined 50 experimental projects and 20 actual pilot programs costing upwards of $100 million over the next eight years.
>
> It was an explosive subject, up [through] the 1970s but, after 1977, EnMod interest seemed to disappear almost overnight. In other words, after decades of intense research and development, after billions of dollars of investment, after major institutions and governmental bodies were created and charged with oversight of EnMod and its many peripheral issues, and after the entire reorganization of the u.s. government to channel and guide and map out the future of this new and promising military and civilian "technology"—said to be more important than the atom bomb—everything stopped.
>
> Or did it? It was as if a huge curtain fell over the subject as all research, all institutional interests, huge salaries and thousands of jobs—vanished. And the mass media stopped reporting anything and everything as if struck by plague. That—sudden and total silence—is perhaps the most telling and suspicious indication of the secrecy and denial that the EnMod arena was shackled with. Today it is almost as if it never happened.

Could it be that the U.S. government said, "Oh gee, we can't do that any more," and just gave up on military EnMod—or did the whole program go "black"?

Project Popeye

The American military-industrial-academic complex early on recognized the importance of weather as a weapon. After the great battles of the Civil War it was noted that rains seems to follow. A General patented an idea for making rain from this observation, but it would take nearly eighty years for a technology to be developed that was GI friendly. The Battle for Britain was partially won because Allied forces successfully used a fog-dispersal system known as FIDO to enable aircraft takeoff and landing under otherwise debilitating fog conditions. Cold fogs were similarly dissipated during the Korean War. Cloud seeding became a weapon in Vietnam under Project Popeye.

Project Popeye is a now exposed and proven conspiracy on the part of the military to circumvent the laws of humanity in time of war using environmental modification as a weapon—and to keep this secret, the Secretary of Defense was forced to lie to Congress.

Project Popeye was originally conducted as a pilot program in 1966. It was an attempt to extend the monsoon season in Southeast Asia with the goal of slowing traffic on the Ho Chi Minh trail by seeding clouds above it in hopes of producing impassable mud. Over the course of the program, silver iodide was dispersed from C-130s, F4 Phantoms and the Douglas A-1E Skyraider (a single-engine propeller-driven fighter-bomber) into clouds over portions of the trail winding from North Vietnam through Laos and Cambodia into South Vietnam. Positive results from the initial test led to continued operations from 1967 through 1972.

Some scientists believe that it did hamper North Vietnamese operations, even though the effectiveness of this program is still in dispute. In 1978, after the efforts at cloud seeding in Vietnam produced mixed results, the U.S. Air Force declared its position to be that "weather modification has little utility as a weapon of war." Recent military publications indeed have stated quite the opposite. For example, the U.S. Air Force's own Air University's "SpaceCast 2020" contained a section on Counterforce Weather Control for force enhancement, which pointed out that:

> Atmospheric scientists have pursued terrestrial weather modification in earnest since the 1940s, but have made little progress because of scientific, legal, and social concerns, as well as certain controls at various government levels. Using environmental modification techniques to destroy, damage, or injure another state are prohibited. However, space presents us with a new arena, technology provides new opportunities, and our conception of future capabilities compels a reexamination of this sensitive and potentially risky topic.

"SpaceCast 2020" has been superseded by the now infamous "Air Force 2025" series of White Papers, which made this same point, saying:

> The influence of the weather on military operations has long been recognized. During World War II, Eisenhower said, "In Europe, bad weather is the worst enemy of the air [operations]. Some soldier once said, 'The weather is always neutral.' Nothing could be more untrue.
>
> Bad weather is obviously the enemy of the side that seeks to launch projects requiring good weather, or of the side possessing great assets, such as strong air forces, which depend upon good weather for effective operations. If really bad weather should endure permanently, the Nazi would need nothing else to defend the Normandy coast!"

Clearly, weather control could have a marked effect on the outcome of military operations. The problem the military has is not whether weather control should be affected, but how it could be done, meaning technically, legally, and politically. Many researchers, myself included, believe that the DOD never truly gave up trying to find out.

Project Popeye reached broad public consciousness when syndicated columnist Jack Anderson revealed it under the code name "In-

termediary-Compatriot" in his *Washington Post* column of 18 March
1971. U.S. Defense Secretary Melvin Laird was forced to testify before
Congress about it in 1972. He told the U.S. Senate that Anderson's wild
tales were untrue and that the United States never tried to seed clouds
in Southeast Asia. But, on 28 January 1974, a private letter from Laird
was leaked to the press. By 1974, he had left Defense and was counsel
to President Nixon who was fighting for his political life following the
break-in at the Democratic Party's National Committee offices in the
Watergate Hotel on 17 June 1972. In the letter, Laird privately admitted that his 1972 testimony had been false and that the U.S. did in fact
use weather modification in North Vietnam in 1967–68.

On 20 March 1974, the United States Senate held a top secret hearing in which representatives of the military finally admitted to the
existence of Operation Popeye. They conceded that the cloud seeding program had been conducted over neutral Cambodia and Laos
(in violation of international law), as well as both North and South
Vietnam. The testifying Pentagon officials stated that Popeye had
been ongoing from 1966 through 1972 and that at least 2,600 flights
had released over 47,000 units of cloud-seeding materials during the
program, at a total cost for the operation of around $21.6 million.

These hearings also revealed that the U.S. military had attempted
other environmental modifications as well. The U.S. had used massive spraying of chemical herbicides in the hopes of depriving its foes
of both food supplies and shelter. According to analyst L. Juda (from
"Negotiating a Treaty on Environmental Modification Warfare: The
Convention on Environmental Warfare and Its Impact on the Arms
Control Negotiations," published in *International Organization*), the
idea was simple:

> If, as has been suggested, the guerrilla is to his base area as fish are to
> the sea, then the destruction of the sea would kill the fish and the elim-
> ination of the base area with its supports would destroy the guerrilla.

The implications of this operation staggered Senator Claiborne Pell,
a Democrat from Rhode Island. In 1976, he said:

The U.S. and other world powers should sign a treaty to outlaw the tampering with weather as an instrument of war. It may seem far-fetched to think of using weather as a weapon, but I am convinced that the U.S. did in fact use rainmaking techniques as a weapon of war in Southeast Asia. We need a treaty now to prevent such actions—before military leaders of the world start directing storms, manipulating climates and inducing earthquakes against their enemies. It may seem a great leap of imagination to move from an apparent effort by the United States to muddy the Ho Chi Minh trail in Laos by weather modification to such science fiction ideas as unleashing earthquakes, melting the polar ice cap, changing the course of warm ocean currents, or modifying the weather of an adversary's farm belt. But in military technology today's science fiction is tomorrow's strategic reality.

Senator Pell had conducted the Senate hearing in 1972, in which he was lied to by Defense Secretary Laird, and the secret one in 1974 that learned the horrible truth. After these, he became a leading advocate for what became the EnMod Convention. A subcommittee chaired by Minnesota Congressman Donald Fraser did the same in the House of Representatives in 1974 and 1975. Senator Pell did a lot of stumping and article writing to force the world to act. In one article he wrote:

Apart from the sheer horror of the prospect of unbridled environmental warfare, there is, I believe, another compelling reason to ban such action. We know, or should know by now, that no nation can maintain for long a monopoly on new warfare technology. If we can develop weather warfare techniques, so can and will other major powers. Experience has taught us that the weapons that make us feel secure today will make us feel very insecure indeed, when our adversaries possess the same capabilities.

In *The Cooling*[147], Lowell Ponte describes the events that led to the EnMod Convention:

147. Lowell Ponte. *The Cooling: Has the Next Ice Age Already Begun?* Prentice-Hall, 1976.

During a summit meeting between President Nixon and Soviet Premier Leonid Brezhnev on July 3, 1974, the nations agreed to conduct discussions toward a ban on environmental warfare. Before the first of these discussions, set for Moscow in November, got underway, the Soviet Union introduced a resolution before the United Nations General Assembly to ban environmental warfare. When revised, the resolution was passed by the body 102 votes to none. The United States and half a dozen other nations abstained from the vote. Senator Pell suspected that the president felt miffed by the surprise Soviet action, a move that made it appear that the Soviet Union, and not the United States, had taken the lead in trying to ban environmental modification. In fact, the Soviet resolution was similar to one passed by the North Atlantic Assembly in November 1972 and to another, authored by Senator Pell, and passed by an 82 to 10 vote by the United States Senate in July 1973.

Discussion between U.S. and Soviet negotiators resumed in Washington, D.C., on February 24, 1975. On August 21, 1975, the two nations presented their jointly produced draft treaty banning environmental modification as a weapon of war to the thirty-one-nation Geneva Disarmament Conference.

The EnMod Convention was later passed by the United Nations General Assembly and opened for signature in 1977. It came into effect 5 October 1978, when it was certified by the required total of 20 nations. It prohibits the use of techniques that would have widespread, long-lasting or severe effects through deliberate manipulation of natural processes and causing such phenomena as earthquakes, tidal waves and changes in climate and in weather patterns. The treaty was warmly received by most of the international community, the exception being a coalition of American environmental groups who thought that its threshold level of a violation needing to be widespread, long-lasting, or severe was too high. Another complaint was that it does not ban the development of this technology, leaving it open for beneficial techniques to be discovered and employed in the service of mankind. The environmentalists (correctly) believed that the failure to ban research in this field would allow the military to develop technologies that adhered to the letter of the law while violating its spirit, as blatantly detailed in the Air Force White Paper entitled "Weather as a Force Multiplier: Owning the Weather in 2025." Unfortunately for us, the EnMod Convention is a total failure with only 70 nations thus far signatory to it, and it is unenforceable in any realistic sense.

Secret Weather Wars?

Zbigniew Kazimierz Brzezinski, a Polish-American political scientist, geostrategist, and statesman who served as United States National Security Advisor to President Jimmy Carter from 1977 to 1981, wrote in his 1970 book, *Between Two Ages:*

> It is ironic to recall that, in 1878, Friedrich Engels, commenting on the Franco-Prussian War, proclaimed that "weapons used have reached such a stage of perfection that further progress which would have any revolutionizing influence is no longer possible." Not only have new weapons been developed, but some of the basic concepts of geography and strategy have been fundamentally altered; space and weather control have replaced Suez or Gibraltar as key elements of strategy.

After events like the Christmas 2004 Asian tsunami and 2005's record-shattering Atlantic hurricane season, many people have wondered just how "natural" those natural disasters were. Has "weather control" really become a key element of national strategy?

In the post-EnMod U.S. of the 21st century, weather control is an activity mainly confined to local governments and privately owned commercial enterprises ("civilian contractors") like Weather Modification, Inc. (WMI) of Fargo, North Dakota. WMI provides services to universities, governmental agencies and private sector entities across the country and around the world. These services include hail suppression in Argentina, snowpack augmentation in Idaho, and cloud seeding in Nevada. Interestingly, one of the senior scientists at WMI went on Art Bell's *Coast To Coast* AM radio show in 2005 to "out" himself as having been one of the scientists involved in Operation Popeye!

Intentional hostile control of the weather and other environmental processes is collectively called geophysical warfare. Dr. Gordon J. F. MacDonald wrote: "The key to geophysical warfare is the identification of environmental instabilities to which the addition of a small amount of energy would release vastly greater amounts of energy." This was in "Geophysical Warfare: How to Wreck the Environment," a chapter he contributed to Nigel Calder's book, *Unless Peace Comes: A Scientific Forecast of New Weapons*.[148]

In the 1960s, Dr. Gordon J. F. MacDonald was a distinguished geophysicist and climatologist. He was Associate Director of the Institute of Geophysics and Planetary Physics at the University of California, Los Angeles (UCLA). Dr. MacDonald was also a member of the President's Science Advisory Committee and the President's Council on Environmental Quality, as well as being a senior member of NASA's first Physics Committee. He was also a member of the Council on Foreign Relations and one of the JASON's, a military think-tank at the top of the military-industrial-academic pyramid.

Dr. MacDonald wrote many articles on future weapons. In "Space," an article for the book *Toward the Year 2018*,[149] Dr. MacDonald elaborated on the possibilities of geophysical warfare, writing:

> … technology will make available to the leaders of the major nations a variety of techniques for conducting secret warfare… Techniques of weather modification could be employed to produce prolonged periods of drought or storm, thereby weakening a nation's capacity and forcing it to accept the demands of the competitor.

Elsewhere he wrote:

148. N. Calder. *Unless Peace Comes: A Scientific Forecast of New Weapons*. A. Lane, 1968.
149. Foreign Policy Association. *Toward the Year 2018*. Cowles Education Corp., 1968.

Such a secret war need never be declared or even known by the affected population. It would go on for years with only the security forces involved being aware of it. The years of drought and storm would be attributed to unkindly nature, and only after a nation was thoroughly drained would an armed takeover be attempted.

He warned that these geophysical weapons systems, should they in fact be developed, would produce long-term upsets in the climate. *Business Week* magazine reported on 24 October 2005:

> China has 35,000 people engaged in weather management, and it spends $40 million a year on alleviating droughts or stemming hail that would damage crops.

North Korea, downwind of China, has been ravaged by droughts for a decade. It is entirely possible that China has been intentionally stealing North Korea's rain so as to force North Korea to follow China's political dictates and buy Chinese food. Reports from North Korea make not just the nation's dictator, Kim Jong-un, but the whole country sound crazy. Could their seeming mass insanity be induced?

HAARP

One much discussed project that embodies both civilian and military geophysical applications is HAARP—the High Frequency Active Auroral Research Program.

Although HAARP proponents claim it is nothing more than a simple civilian research station designed to investigate the properties of the upper atmosphere, few investigators buy that explanation.

HAARP does have the appearance of a civilian project with open access and the work being done by civilian scientists. However, the project is managed by a joint U.S. Air Force and Navy committee and is funded out of the Department of Defense (DOD) budget.

Most recently, the heart of the program, the Ionospheric Research Instrument (IRI), was completed by one of the world's largest defense contractors working under the direction of the Defense Advanced

Research Projects Agency (DARPA), a top research and development (R&D) organization for the DOD.

DARPA manages and directs selected basic and applied R&D projects for the DOD pursuing research and technology "where risk and payoff are both very high and where success may provide dramatic advances for traditional military roles and missions."

Under construction since 1990, the HAARP IRI is a field of antennas on the ground in southeast Alaska. The facility was probably completed late in 2005 with the announcement of same added to the DARPA website in March of 2006. It is now the world's largest radio frequency (RF) broadcaster, with an effective radiated power of 3.6 million watts—over 72,000 times more powerful than the largest single AM radio station in the United States (50,000 watts).

The IRI uses a unique patented ability to focus the RF energy generated by the field, injecting it into a spot at the very top of the atmosphere in a region called the ionosphere. This heats the thin atmosphere of the ionospheric region by several thousand degrees. HAARP, then, is a type of device called an ionospheric heater.

This heating allows scientists to do a number of things with the ionosphere. Controlling and directing the processes and forces of the ionosphere is called "ionospheric enhancement." An early HAARP document stated:

> The heart of the program will be the development of a unique ionospheric heating capability to conduct the pioneering experiments required to adequately assess the potential for exploiting ionospheric enhancement technology for DOD purposes.

What might those DOD purposes be? Something about winning wars, eh? How might those purposes be achieved? What technologies will be needed to win the wars of the future? Researchers trying to answer those questions have come up with a vast number of possibilities, most bordering on science fiction. But then again, good science fiction is about recognizing the problems of the future and suggesting solutions to them before they happen.

On 23 March 1983, President Ronald Reagan called upon "the scientific community in our country, those who gave us nuclear weapons, to turn their great talents now to the cause of mankind and world peace, to give us the means of rendering these nuclear weapons impotent and obsolete."

This quest for the creation of a technology, of a weapon or weapons system that would make atomic war impossible, was officially named the Strategic Defense Initiative (SDI). The press lost no time in dubbing it "Star Wars" after the George Lucas movie.

That initiative sent the United States military-industrial-academic complex on the greatest and costliest weapons hunt in human history. Thousands of ideas were floated, hundreds of those were funded. While SDI research has since been officially abandoned, some ideas are still being actively pursued to this day.

Not all of these ongoing developmental programs are taking place in laboratories of the military and its contractors. Some of these ideas involve technologies or applications that, as weapons, violate international treaties and/or would be repugnant to the ethical and moral values of the majority of Americans. In an effort to avoid public outcry (and international condemnation), some of these programs have been disguised as civilian science. One of those may be HAARP.

As Dr. Bernard Eastlund, the putative inventor of HAARP, put it: "The boundary between science fiction and science comes with can you actually make the thing that you're proposing."

Bernard J. Eastlund is a physicist who received his BS in physics from MIT and his PHD in physics from Columbia University. He led a team of scientists and engineers working for Advanced Power Technologies, Inc. (APTI), a wholly owned subsidiary of ARCO.

Eastlund's team developed the concept of a massive antenna array that could produce the kind of shield called for by President Reagan.

The APTI patents that HAARP is probably based on openly discuss manipulating the weather by moving the jet stream and using other techniques to create floods and droughts at will. These patents also describe a way to raise the ionosphere, sending it out into space as an electrically charged plasma capable of destroying anything electronic (like an incoming ICBM or a spy satellite) passing through it. HAARP certainly looks like a ground-based "Star Wars" weapons system, a relic of the Cold War. But unlike most such relics, this one is up and running and stays fully funded.

In August of 2002, the Russian State Duma (their version of Congress or Parliament) expressed concern about HAARP, calling it a program to develop "a qualitatively new type of weapon." A joint commission of the State Duma's International Affairs and Defense Committees issued a report that said:

> Under the High Frequency Active Auroral Research Program (HAARP) the USA is creating new integral geophysical weapons that may influence the near-Earth medium with high frequency radio waves. The significance of this qualitative leap could be compared to the transition from cold steel to firearms, or from conventional weapons to nuclear weapons. This new type of weapon differs from previous types in that the near-Earth medium becomes at once an object of direct influence and its component.

The report further claimed that the USA's plan to carry out large-scale scientific experiments under the HAARP program, and not controlled by the global community, would create weapons capable of jamming radio communications, disrupting equipment installed on spaceships and rockets, provoke serious accidents in electricity networks and in oil and gas pipelines and have a negative impact on the mental health of people populating entire regions. An appeal, signed by 90 deputies, demanding that an international ban be put on such large-scale geophysical experiments, was sent to President Vladimir Putin, to the United Nations and other international organizations, to the parliaments and leaders of the U.N. member countries, to the scientific public and to mass media outlets.

Getting back to Dr. MacDonald. Among the coming "advances" he wrote about were manipulation or control over the weather and climate, including destructive use of ocean waves and melting or destabilizing of the polar ice caps, intentional ozone depletion, triggering earthquakes, and control of the human brain by utilizing the Earth's energy fields.

Today, the polar ice caps are indeed melting and holes in the ozone layer are growing. Could these be the handiwork of advanced weapons? What about earthquakes and mind control? Are we, the private citizens of the world, in the crosshairs of bizarre, unthinkable weapons?

What about the Russian Duma's claim that HAARP could have a negative impact on the mental health of people populating entire regions of the globe? In "Vandalism In The Sky," their seminal article on HAARP in *Nexus Magazine*, Dr. Nick Begich and Jeane Manning describe how HAARP could be used to induce mental dysfunction, quoting from Brzezinski on a proposal from Dr. MacDonald, saying:

> Political strategists are tempted to exploit research on the brain and human behavior. Geophysicist Gordon J. F. MacDonald—specialist in problems of warfare—says [an] accurately-timed, artificially-excited electronic stroke "could lead to a pattern of oscillations that produce relatively high power levels over certain regions of the Earth… In this way, one could develop a system that would seriously impair the brain performance of very large populations in selected regions over an extended period…"

Dr. MacDonald commented on the possible use of the destructive effects of electromagnetic fields in the environment on human health and performance. He said that weapons systems could be developed that would increase the intensity of the electromagnetic field oscillating in the spherical-shaped cavity between the Earth and the ionosphere and that these weapons could be used to "seriously impair brain performance in very large populations in selected regions over an extended period," just as the Duma feared HAARP might do. Could HAARP, or another similar antenna elsewhere, be the source of North Korea's madness? Could Kim Jong-un be a true "Manchurian candidate"? And if so, whose?

In 1969, Dr. MacDonald wrote:

Our understanding of basic environmental science and technology is primitive, but still more primitive are our notions of the proper political forms and procedures to deal with the consequences of modification.

It would appear that the gap between our understanding of environmental science and technology and our ability to grapple with this knowledge as a body politic has changed little in the intervening decades. You, my friend, must take action to create the necessary "forms and procedures to deal with the consequences of modification." It is, after all, *your* planet.

Published in issue 4 of The Dot Connector Magazine
(July-August 2009).

About the authors

○ **H. P. Albarelli, Jr.**, is an American investigative reporter and writer. His works have been translated into 16 languages. Following a ten-year investigation, his book, *A Terrible Mistake: The Murder of Frank Olson and the CIA's Secret Cold War Experiments*, was published by Trine Day in January 2010. For more information, visit *aterriblemistake.com*.

○ **Walter H. Bowart** (1939–2007) was an American leader in the counterculture movement of the 1960s, founder and editor of the first underground newspaper in New York City, the *East Village Other*, and the author of the bestselling book *Operation Mind Control* (Dell, 1978).

○ **Jüri Lina** was born in 1949 in Estonia. In 1979, emigrated to Sweden, after repeated conflicts with the Soviet political police, KGB, which regarded him as one of the most anti-Communist writers. Jüri is the author of the books *Under the Sign of the Scorpion: The Rise and Fall of the Soviet Empire* (3rd ed., 2014) and *Architects of Deception: The Concealed History of Freemasonry* (2004).

○ **Michael Nield** is a British researcher, author of the highly recommended book *The Police State Road Map* (self-published; 2nd ed., 2005).

○ **Ron Patton** is an American conspiracy and mind control researcher, author and publisher of *Paranoia Magazine*, which he revived from dormancy with a Summer 2012 hard copy issue. Read more about him at *paranoiamagazine.com*.

○ **Hans Ruesch** (1913–2007) was a Swiss medical historian, novelist, and internationally prominent activist against animal experiments and vivisection as well as against profit motives of the medical-pharmaceutical industry.

○ **Jerry E. Smith** (1950–2010) was an American author, researcher, poet and editor. His bibliography includes the books *Weather Warfare: The Mil-*

itary's Plan to Draft Mother Nature (2006); *HAARP: The Ultimate Weapon of the Conspiracy* (1998); and *Secrets of the Holy Lance: The Spear of Destiny in History & Legend* (2005, with George Piccard), all from Adventures Unlimited Press.

o **DICK SUTPHEN** is the author of 21 books, one of which, *You Were Born Again to Be Together* (1976), became a million-copy bestseller. Dick has a private hypnotherapy practice and trained thousands of people to become professional hypnotists. His radio show on *BlogTalkRadio*, "Dick Sutphen's Metaphysical World, Spiritual Concepts," is heard by nearly half a million people a week. His website is at *dicksutphen.org.*

o **DANI VERACITY** is a citizen journalist, a *NaturalNews.com* reporter, and the author (with Mike Adams) of the books *Natural Appetite Suppressants for Safe, Effective Weight Loss* and *The Real Safety Guide to Disease Prevention* (both Truth Publishing Int'l, 2011).

o **WALTER C. VETSCH** was born in 1947 in Louisiana with a gift that he himself defines as the "unlearned knowledge." From his earliest years, he knew exactly what "reality" really was, how it worked, and what were the forces that made it work. "All that I write," Walter says, "is based on the material I was able to bring through from before I was born here." His printed books are *TEXT* (2015) and *Playthings of the gods* (2015, a collection of 11 essays & novels). His website is at *3108.info.*

Index

Printed in Great Britain
by Amazon